Studying Creatively

Are you stuck in a rut? Short of inspiration? Looking for a study guide that's a break from the norm?

This innovative book will give you the tools and techniques you need to work a bit of creative magic into every aspect of your studying.

Brian Clegg's easy-to-read, entertaining book will show you:

- what the whole creativity business is about;
- why you need to bother with it;
- clever methods to stimulate your brain into action;
- how to come up with a mass of ideas at a moment's notice.

Mind stretches and mental workouts will enable you to take effective notes and to absorb and structure information in a way that can easily be recalled.

It's also very important to be relaxed and comfortable (though not too relaxed and comfortable, or you'll end up asleep). *Studying Creatively* will show you how to change your environment to make creative study more effective.

This study guide with a difference will help you work on your presentation skills – there's no point having great ideas if you can't put them across.

Good ideas are essential for any student who wants to do well. This invaluable guide empowers you with the tools you need to work creatively, and shows that creativity isn't just about getting good results, it's fun and gives you a real buzz.

Brian Clegg is a fellow of the Royal Society for the Encouragement of Arts, Manufactures and Commerce and has a company, Creativity Unleashed, to help large organizations be more creative. He now specialises in writing popular science and speaks regularly at venues from schools to science festivals.

Studying Creatively

A creativity toolkit to get
your studies out of a rut

Brian Clegg

Routledge
Taylor & Francis Group

LONDON AND NEW YORK

First published 2008
by Routledge
2 Park Square, Milton Park, Abingdon, Oxon OX14 4RN

Simultaneously published in the USA and Canada
by Routledge
270 Madison Ave, New York, NY 10016

Routledge is an imprint of the Taylor & Francis Group, an informa business

© 2008 Brian Clegg

Typeset in Garamond and Gill Sans
by Keystroke, High Street, Tettenhall, Wolverhampton
Printed and bound in Great Britain
by TJ International Ltd, Padstow, Cornwall

British Library Cataloguing in Publication Data
A catalogue record for this book is available from the British Library

Library of Congress Cataloging in Publication Data
Clegg, Brian.
Studying creatively : a creativity toolkit to get your studies out
of a rut / Brian Clegg.
p. cm.
Includes bibliographical references and index.
1. Study skills. 2. Creative thinking. I. Title.
LB1049.C5497 2007
371.3′0281—dc22
2007003143

ISBN10: 0–415–42814–9 (hbk)
ISBN10: 0–415–42815–7 (pbk)
ISBN10: 0–203–94555–7 (ebk)

ISBN13: 978–0–415–42814–9 (hbk)
ISBN13: 978–0–415–42815–6 (pbk)
ISBN13: 978–0–203–94555–1 (ebk)

For Gillian, Chelsea and Rebecca

Contents

Acknowledgements   xi

1 Why creativity?   1

What's the point? 1
Can you do anything? 3
Getting the technique 5
The brain, the whole brain, and nothing but the brain 6
Under pressure 10
Why creativity? – essentials 11

2 Mind magic   12

Making it happen 12
But first, the bad news 12
Trampling the little green shoots 14
What makes you an expert? 14
I'm scared 15
Touch of wow! 15
Take a hike 16
Random Picture 17
Attributes 23
Reversal 25
Being someone else 27
Getting a boost 29
Taking off the wheel nuts 30
More techniques and free software 31
Giving the brain a workout 31
Puzzles, problems and mind stretching 32
Mind Stretch 1: Get the sandwich 33

Mind Stretch 2: Three in quick succession 34
Mind Stretch 3: The magic mix 36
Mind Stretch 4: The missing bullet 37
Mind Stretch 5: A girdle round about the earth 38
Mind Stretch 6: The great escape 39
Mind Stretch 7: Three more quickies 40
Mental Workout 1: Hiding a secret 41
Mental Workout 2: Make it a metaphor 43
Mental Workout 3: It's story time 44
Mental Workout 4: Seeing is beleafing 45
Mental Workout 5: Let the story find you 46
Mind magic – essentials 46

3 An original approach 48

Personal without the weird 48
Building your structure 49
Hold the layout 52
Picture this 54
A font of knowledge 55
Being very bold 56
Colouring in 58
Drawing them in 60
On paper; on screen 63
An original approach – essentials 65

4 Mapping the facts 66

Why take notes? 66
Kicking the brain into action 67
Layout, highlight, illustrate 68
Going to the next level: mind maps 69
Hitting the category 71
Is writing necessary? 72
Doing it on the computer 73
Mapping the facts – essentials 76

5 Memories are made of this 78

Brains aren't computers 79
Pick a number, any number 80
What is this garbage? 81

Here's one I remembered earlier 82
Numbers have shapes too 85
I want to tell you a story 86
Your brain in chains 87
Do it out loud, write it, draw it 87
I know the face, but what's the name? 89
Recap and recap . . . and recap again 91
Will I run out of space? 92
The 'can't be bothered' phenomenon 93
Memories are made of this – essentials 93

6   Read for speed   95

Back to basics 95
In a flash 97
Sinking in 97
Screening your work 98
Hunting for essentials 99
Read for speed – essentials 101

7   Chill out   102

My brain time 102
Where and when am I creative? 104
Balancing pressure 105
Natural medication 107
Destress 1: Get some sleep and some good food 107
Destress 2: Get on top of your time 109
Destress 3: Get some air 109
Destress 4: Get a laugh 110
Destress 5: Get physical 111
Destress 6: Get a winner's trophy 112
Destress 7: Get a list 113
Destress 8: Get a conversation 114
Destress 9: Get offloaded 115
Destress 10: Get some relaxation 116
Chill out – essentials 117

8   Time and time again   119

How much time? 119
How long at one go? 121

Dealing with distractions 123
Give yourself a medal 124
What comes first? 125
Top Ten 126
Finding loose time 127
Saying 'no' 129
Expect the unexpected 129
Time and time again – essentials 131

9   **Creativity zone**   133

Remember the wheel nuts 133
10 a.m. – time to be creative 133
Take charge of your time 135
Change the way you take notes 135
Look for creativity triggers 136
Take another look at your presentation 136
Read more, but read differently 137
Make sure you are chilling out 137
Studying creatively 138

Appendix: Creativity resources   139

Creativity online 139
Books to help with creativity 140
Creativity software 140
Puzzles, problems and mind stretching 140
More on a different kind of reading 141
Observations 141

Index   147

Acknowledgements

Thanks to Philip Mudd, Lucy Wainwright and Amy Crowle at Taylor & Francis for making writing this book fun.

Chapter 1

Why creativity?

This opening chapter is here to give you some background to what the whole creativity business is about, and why you need to bother with it. If you are the sort of person who skips introductions to get to the real thing, that's fine; I just ask that you hang on in with me for a couple of paragraphs before skipping to Chapter 2. I'll let you know when it's safe to go.

I have been teaching people about creativity for over ten years now – all the way up from junior school children to board members of big companies – and I've found that it helps a lot to get a feeling for what creativity is about, and why the techniques that help you be more creative work, before getting into the detail of what to do to be more creative in your studying. It's partly because some creativity techniques can seem weird unless you know *why* you're doing them, and partly because knowing what the techniques are for, and how they work, will help you know how and when to use the techniques you're going to come across.

OK, now it's up to you. Read on if you want to put those techniques in context (which I'd really recommend); skip to Chapter 2 for the fast track.

What's the point?

One thing is for certain: there's no point wasting your time learning how to be more creative if you aren't going to do anything with it. This isn't one of those boring academic 'learning for the sake of it' subjects; it's a practical skill that's going to be intensely useful in school or university, at work and in your everyday life. It's also a skill that isn't going to lose value over time. It will stick with you for ever.

Creativity lets you do two things: solve problems and come up with new ideas. I tend not to bother too much about the difference between these. You can be solving a problem that amounts to 'I need a new idea', or getting an idea on 'how to solve my problem'. Some creativity experts spend ages agonizing over the difference between the two, or between creativity and innovation. Forget it. Life's too short. As far as I'm concerned, it's all the same thing. Creativity.

It's easy to get stuck with the idea that creativity is about 'the arts'. If you think like that, the closest that creativity gets to the real world is advertising (where some employees are actually referred to as 'creatives'). But creativity is not all about writing literature and painting pictures (and advertising). It's about having ideas, about changing things, about making things happen. And that comes in useful everywhere.

To start with – and I think most importantly – it's a personal thing. Creativity is about doing something original, something that comes from *you* and no one else. There really is nothing that gives the same buzz as being creative. It could be one of those arty things, like writing something or taking a great photograph. But it could equally be thinking of a great new way to make money, or a clever new tactic on the football field, or some way to change your room so it's a better place to be.

As well as helping with these personal issues, creativity is going to be incredibly valuable with your work, whether it's schoolwork or the money-earning kind. It might involve finding a new way to do something (or an entirely new thing do). It might mean coping with a really irritating problem. It could be a way of saving money or beating the competition.

Creativity gurus like to say that creativity is about differentiation. This is just a way of saying that creativity helps you stand out from the crowd (but by using big words like 'differentiation', the guru can charge £300 an hour for telling people). Creativity is a way of making yourself different, or your company different, or what you are different, or what you sell different. And that can result in anything from cheering yourself up to surviving in a life-threatening situation.

If you want the single-phrase summary, you could do worse than say that creativity is what makes life worthwhile. How could anyone doubt there's a point to it?

Can you do anything?

OK, we need creativity, but that doesn't mean that there's any reason to write a book (or to read one) about it. Breathing, for example, is also kind of essential for life, but a whole book on breathing would get dull pretty quickly. Imagine something like this:

The Student's Guide to Breathing

By Brian Clegg

Breathe in. Breathe out. Keep doing it – not too quickly, not too slowly. Don't bother to think about it: your body will look after it.

The End.

It doesn't have the feel of a bestseller. The reason there's not much of a book in breathing is that you don't have a lot of choice, it's just something that happens. If the same were true of creativity, then again the book would be short and not worth spending your money on. The 'natural' approach to being creative, the creativity equivalent of 'just breathe', is waiting for the big light bulb to go on over your head.

Aside: Metaphors

When I talk about a big light bulb going on over your head, I am speaking metaphorically. Unless you are a cartoon character, there is no big light bulb over your head; it just represents an idea arriving. Keep an eye out for metaphors; they're very useful in creativity and we'll come back to them later.

So, on flashes that big light bulb. You sat in your bedroom, or garage, or at your desk and waited . . . and if you were lucky, you eventually had an idea.

That's great if you've got all the time in the world and nothing better to do than sit around waiting. But that doesn't apply to most of us. So, for a long time people have been looking for ways to improve on the basic capabilities of a human brain when it comes to dreaming up ideas, and over the past 50 years a strange collection of people including psychologists, business people and advertising executives (individually – they tend not to talk to each other) have come up with some genuinely effective ways to get systematic about the business of creativity.

Aside: How long is a long time?

It's true that 50 years is a long time, but people have been finding ways to improve on their brain's basic capabilities much longer. Some of the memory techniques mentioned in this book go back to ancient Greek times, while Leonardo da Vinci had a way of dreaming up new ideas that involved drawing squiggles with his eyes shut, then looking at the squiggles and imagining what they could be. (No one said it was a *good* way, but then he was Leonardo, so his squiggles were worth taking a look at.)

Altogether, I've found five different ways you can improve on the creativity of the brains you begin with. They are:

- **Culture** – no, I'm still not talking about the arts. This is the culture of where you live and work (or go to school or university if you don't consider that working). If you are somewhere that supports new ideas and helps you try them out, then you are more likely to be creative than if the typical response to a new idea is 'keep quiet and get on with what you were supposed to be doing'.
- **Techniques** – these are clever little methods to stimulate your brain into action. As they're probably the least ordinary of the five ways, I'll come back to them separately in a moment.
- **Environment** – where you are and how you feel can make a lot of difference to how good your ideas are. It's much easier to get good ideas when you are relaxed and comfortable (though not too relaxed and comfortable, or you'll end up asleep).

- **Practice** – this is life's way of telling you there's no such thing as a free lunch. We all start off with different abilities, but most of them get better with practice, and creativity is just like playing tennis or driving a car in this respect. The more opportunity you get to try out techniques and to come up with new ideas, the easier it becomes to fire off a pile of ideas at a moment's notice.
- **Fun** – there's a strong link between creativity and fun. That's not to say that as long as you're having fun you are being creative; just having a great time with your friends doesn't mean you are oozing creativity. But if you are being creative you are likely to be having fun, and if you are in a place where fun is frowned on, it can be hard to be creative.

By working on these five aspects, anyone can get more creative. Some folk will tell you that there are creative people and the rest. (And most of the world falls into the 'the rest' category, though, interestingly, people who have this theory almost always put themselves into the elite creative people group.) Don't listen to these 'the common rabble aren't capable of creative thinking' types. It's true that some people find it easier than others to come up with really great ideas, but everyone is capable of fresh thinking, and everyone can get better at creativity with the right techniques, environment and plenty of practice.

Getting the technique

This book uses techniques a lot, so it's worth getting an idea of what they are and why they work. There are some specialist mind techniques, like those we use to help remember things better, but most creativity techniques are ways of getting you to look at things differently and make new connections in your brain.

New connections are essentially what ideas are. Your brain is a huge network of interconnected links – new ideas come from setting up different connections, a bit like putting someone through on one of those mechanical telephone switchboards you sometimes see on old movies. (This is a metaphor too! The brain is a lot more complicated than this.) Generally we like to do things in a certain way. We're comfortable with it. It's what we know works. But it's a bit like being in a tunnel. You don't just get tunnel vision, you're living in this tunnel. You can only go places that are inside the tunnel.

The tunnel for your ideas is formed by all the assumptions you make about how things are in the world. That's fine if you can come up with an idea that's in your tunnel, but most of them won't be. They'll be out there, in the big wide world outside the tunnel. Techniques are pickaxes to break out of tunnel vision caused by your assumptions and lack of original thought.

You'll sometimes hear people saying, 'We need to think outside the box'. That's just another way to say break out of the tunnel, but it has been mocked so often on TV shows that it's best not to use it unless you are being ironic.

The strange thing about techniques is that they're mechanical. You just follow a set of instructions – often very simple instructions – and, magically, new ideas are created. Some people find this very strange. How can anything as wonderful and human as creativity be mechanical? The point is, it's not the technique that does the creating, it's you. The mechanical part is just a matter of knocking some barriers down – then the brain kicks in and does the real work.

Creativity techniques are used a lot in teams, especially at work. Most of this book will be giving you ideas on how to be creative on your own, but a lot of the stuff in here will also work for teams or committees or groups of friends. There are a few techniques that are really only relevant to groups. Probably the best-known creativity technique is brainstorming, which is intended for a group of people. Where necessary we'll bring group techniques in – but the main thing is to remember that ideas come to individual people. Groups are great at improving ideas and combining them to make new ones, but that first spark of originality has to come from someone. Make sure you get some thinking time alone, even if you are working with a team.

The brain, the whole brain, and nothing but the brain

Not only does an idea come from a single person, it comes from a single organ in the body. There's no point trying to be creative with your liver; it won't get you anywhere. This is brain work, pure and simple. Because of that, it helps to get to know a little bit about the brain, which we'll do without getting into *too* much gruesome detail.

The brain is a complex device, and one that doesn't come with a user manual. A very simplistic way of looking at the brain is to see it as a series of switches, rather like the bits in a computer. You have around 10 billion of these biological switches called neurons – in computer-speak, 10 giganeurons. That might not sound so much, but the comparison is based on an enormous error. The brain isn't anything like a computer. One of the big differences between brains and computers is that, unlike computer bits, each neuron is capable of interaction with hundreds or thousands of others. The way you can combine 10 billion things together, each potentially linking to hundreds of thousands of others, is astronomically huge. We're talking more configurations than there are atoms in the universe. Just to give an idea of how much connectivity there is in there, the dendrites that link the neurons in your brain are the equivalent of having around 93,000 miles of wiring in your head. That's wiring that would stretch around the world four times.

It doesn't do any harm in trying to use your brain more effectively to be aware of its limitations and give it a spot of pampering. One simple way to get better ideas is to be aware that your brain isn't at its best every waking minute of the day. Everyone has times when they are better or worse with the brain (we'll come back to this in more detail later on). Most of us aren't too good at thinking effectively just after a heavy meal. The brain is a big consumer of blood, and when the stomach is making heavy demands on the circulatory system, the brain isn't always at its sharpest.

Most people aren't too bright when they are really tired, either – so last thing at night often isn't best. (Incidentally, this is nothing to do with falling asleep. When you are half asleep you often have some of your best ideas. The brain is better at making new connections when it can operate slowly, drifting from place to place, so a daydreaming state is a good one for having ideas.)

There's something else you should know about your brain: you've got two of them. A slight exaggeration, but not a huge one. You've seen pictures of the brain – it's not unlike an enormous walnut in appearance. The two halves of the brain you see divided by a line down the middle are totally separate all the way down to the corpus callosum, a bundle of nerves linking the brain to the spinal cord right at its base. Broadly speaking, the two sides of the brain control the opposite sides of the body. The left side of your brain is responsible for your right eye, right hand, and so on. (Some animals have even greater functional separation. A dolphin, for example, can sleep on one side of the brain at a time while the other side keeps alert to make sure everything's OK.)

However, one thing you can be sure of with the brain: just when you thought you understood it, it turns out be more complicated than you realized. For example, the idea of a left/right split in the brain is only partly true. Your right eye is also connected to the right side of the brain (though with fewer connections than go to the left). This cross-connection is used to compare the information from the two eyes, to help sort out distances in 3D vision. Some animals have much less cross-connection; their eyes act pretty well independently, and they don't worry too much about how far away things are.

This left/right divide was for a long time thought to be responsible for two very different ways your brain works. The left-hand side was said to be responsible for logical work, handling lists and words and numbers, taking a step-by step, systematic approach. The right side, on the other hand, looked after colour, images, locating things in space, art and taking the overview. It was, like, holistic, man.

This too has proved over-simplistic. Both physical sides of the brain are active in the two modes of operation, even if one dominates. But there definitely are two distinct modes. You can even test this out yourself with something called the Stroop effect.

Aside: Doing the Stroop

The Stroop effect, named after a Dutch psychologist rather than some nasty disease, is a simple way to enable people to actually feel their brains changing gear as they switch from one mode of thinking to the other. It's something anyone can try with a few sheets of paper or, even better, with a PowerPoint presentation.

On each sheet of paper, or PowerPoint slide, write a word. (You can combine all the words on one slide if you make each word appear separately.) The word should be the name of a colour. Keep it relatively simple – say six to eight distinct colours. The first few words should be printed in the same colour as the word says. After that, the word should be printed in a different colour. So if, in the following example, the colour the word is printed in is in [square brackets], then red [green] means the word 'red' printed in the colour green, your sequence might go something like this:

- red   [red]
- blue   [blue]
- orange   [orange]
- purple   [purple]
- orange   [orange]
- blue   [blue]
- green   [green]
- red   [red]
- blue   [green]
- purple   [red]
- green   [purple]
- . . .

. . . and so on. Get a group of people to shout out the colour the word is printed in, as you show them the word. Go through them at a reasonable pace. Even though you've told them to say the colour it's printed in, very soon the left brain will take over and be reading the word. When you suddenly hit 'blue' printed in green, they really will feel their brains struggling to switch mode. After a few more words (how many depends on the individual) their brain will settle into right brain action – but before then they will feel that switch very noticeably.

When we're studying, or otherwise working on something, unless it is very visual the temptation is to rely mostly on what's still called 'left brain thinking' even if both sides of the brain are involved. And that's a problem if we are trying to be creative, because to make new connections we want as much of the brain active as possible. That's why a lot of creativity exercises tend to give the right-hand side a push by using colour and visuals and spatial thinking. It all helps to make sure you are making the most of your brain.

Aside: How much brain do you use?

For many years it was popular to tell people that they only used a fraction of their brain. I confess to having fallen for this one myself. A book I wrote back in 1999 called *Instant Brainpower* solemnly says, 'there is no doubt the brain is underworked. Estimates of the percentage usage vary from the conservative 10% to as little as 0.1% – whatever the true value, there is vast overcapacity.'

It later turned out that someone had made these numbers up with no scientific basis whatsoever. Modern medical scanners can follow just what the brain is doing at any one time, and there's no question of 90 per cent of it sitting idle. It's firing on all cylinders. What *is* true is that we use only a fraction of its capability (as opposed to capacity). Our brains can do a lot more than they normally do. But it's not a question of only being partially used.

Under pressure

As well as finding ways to use your brain better, it's important to be aware that there are things out there that can stop your brain working so effectively. Mostly it comes down to pressure – overload. If you want your brain to do its stuff, you need to do two things: remove the conscious distractions and reduce any stress.

If you think about when people have their best ideas – usually out for a walk, in the bath, in bed; hardly ever sitting at their desk working (or in meetings) – it's obvious that distractions don't help. You can't come up with good ideas when you are bombarded with chat, being asked to do three other things or generally being too mentally active.

There is one special case, though, which is a background activity. Many people find this actually helps them have ideas. It can be listening to music, driving a car, even having the TV on if you aren't really concentrating on it. These background activities help your mind indulge in the daydreaming state that is best for coming up with new ideas. But they don't work for everyone. Some people can't cope with music (say) in the background; it always catches their attention. If you are engaged enough with what you are hearing to sing along to it, you are too conscious of it. This really is one where whatever works for you is best. If having music on helps you think, play it. If not, go for silence. There is no right answer.

The stress thing is related, but a bit different. By stress, I don't mean having a reasonable deadline. Many people have their best ideas when they know they've got to get something sorted out today. But time pressure (or any other sort of pressure) that gets you worried or panicking is very bad for creativity. This is both because your mind starts leaping all over the place and can't come up with a concrete idea, and because when the pressure's on, the mechanisms of the brain automatically choose well-trodden paths. Your brain can't cope with new ideas when it's under pressure.

Why creativity? – essentials

Let's have a quick reminder of what has been covered:

- We need creativity to make ourselves different, to come up with new ideas and to solve problems.
- Creativity isn't just about getting good results, it's fun and gives you a real buzz.
- It's possible to improve your creativity, using:

  - *culture* – not always being down on people who have new ideas;
  - *techniques* – to help you to see things differently;
  - *environment* – because the way you feel influences how good your ideas are;
  - *practice* – creativity gets better with experience;
  - *fun* – just because you are having fun, that doesn't mean you are being creative, but when you are, you will have fun.

- Techniques have been developed, mostly over the past 50 years, to act as a pickaxe to break out of your tunnel.
- You need to use all your brain if possible, so aspects like colour, visual images and spatial thinking will help if added to the usual structured approach when doing school or business work.
- Pressure isn't good for creativity. Get away from it all and relax (without falling asleep!) to get good ideas.

Chapter 2

Mind magic

Making it happen

Later on we will look at ways of presenting your ideas, giving them structure, getting more into memory, dealing with your time, and more. But the starting point is having the ideas themselves. Creativity is about coming up with ideas and solving problems. We've seen that techniques have been developed over the past 50 years to help anyone who needs an idea – whether it's for an essay topic, designing a new product for a technology project, solving a problem at school or coming up with the great new internet business that will make you a multimillionaire. This chapter will give you an introduction to these techniques, so you can boost production in your own mental idea factory.

There will be some examples for you to try out later in the chapter. Please do so. Remember, creativity is improved by practice. If you don't try out these techniques, it will be a lot harder to use them when you really need them.

But first, the bad news

Before we get on to the techniques, though, there's a barrier to be overcome. People are good at blocking creativity. You need to know how they do it before you go out there and have great ideas, so you can spot the blocking in action and do something about it.

The person most often responsible for blocking your creativity is likely to be someone very close to you. In fact, it is you. Most of us are really good at this. The reason is that we think that we aren't particularly creative. We're no good at coming up with ideas. And because of this, we won't be creative. It's sometimes called a self-fulfilling prophecy or the Pygmalion effect. The process is quite simple. Imagine you have a good idea. But you know you aren't any good at this being creative thing. So you think to yourself, 'That idea is useless. It's a joke. I won't tell anyone, or do anything about it, or they'll laugh at me.'

You act as your own worst critic – and switch yourself off. Being criticized is horrible. I know this; I write books, and there's nothing worse than someone coming along after you've spent months sweating over a book, and having them throw together a review that says what you have written is rubbish. This is a genuinely painful experience. Criticism done well is fine – if it's the sort that helps make things better. But much criticism is just negative, and that's typical of what you do to yourself.

As long as you think that your ideas stink, you won't suggest them to anyone, or do anything with them. The first and biggest barrier is realizing that you can have good ideas, and it's worth giving them a try.

Bear in mind, though, that this isn't a magic wand. It won't turn a bad idea into a good one. Simply wanting something doesn't make it happen. If you've ever seen *The X Factor* or *American Idol* on TV you will understand this. A lot of the contestants truly believe they are potential stars, even though their singing is atrocious and they are as attractive as a warthog. They go on (and on) about how much they want it, but that's missing the point. No matter how much they want it, without the talent they aren't going to get it.

Similarly, believing in your own creativity won't make all your ideas good. But some of them will be – and with practice and the techniques below, more of them will be. The important thing, though, is to get your ideas out there and do something with them. This is because an idea you just keep in your head isn't creative. It needs to be put into action. This does mean developing a bit of a thick skin; you need to be able to come up with ideas and be prepared to have some of them fail. Be prepared to be criticized. But hang on to that belief in your ability to think things up.

Once you overcome that first barrier, there are other blockages to creativity to be aware of. These are mostly ones we do to other people, instead of ourselves. This is how we destroy ideas before they have a chance. I'm going to tell you how people do this, not so you can be better at destroying other people's ideas (appealing though this is if they've just torn yours to pieces), but so you can watch out for the occasions when you (and others) do this, and bring attention to this unconsciously destructive behaviour, to give the ideas a chance.

Trampling the little green shoots

After blocking your own ideas, the most common barrier to creativity is attacking an idea too early on. Almost every new idea has faults. They're a bit like little green shoots, just starting to grow in a newly planted lawn. Those shoots are very easy to trample all over and destroy. But encourage them, feed them and give them a chance to grow – then they'll withstand anything you throw at them. It's the same with ideas. When someone first dreams an idea up, it's easy to shoot it down, to moan about it, to say what's wrong with it.

Don't do that. Give a new idea a chance. Build on it and help it to grow. Then you can see whether it's worthwhile, but don't attack it too soon.

What makes you an expert?

Another way of getting heavy on someone else's ideas is to attack their expertise. Again, think of *X Factor* or *American Idol*. Someone gets a 'no'. So they face up to one of the judges (usually Simon Cowell in either show) and say, 'What do you know? You know nothing. Can you sing any better than me? You can't sing. Just you wait; you'll see when I'm a star. You'll regret it!'

The frustrated would-be stars who react like this are making a big mistake. They think you have to be able to sing yourself in order to criticize a singer. Because the judge isn't an 'expert' in their eyes, he doesn't count. Now there's nothing wrong with being an expert. It's great. But you don't have to be able to do the thing you are commenting on to make a useful comment. Similarly, you don't have to be an expert in a subject to come up with a good idea.

In fact, experts are sometimes the worst people to come up with good ideas, because they know what you *can't* do. They're great at telling you what's not possible. And because of the assumptions they make, they're often wrong. The idea for the instant Polaroid camera, for example, didn't come from an engineer or a photographer. People with that kind of expertise knew you couldn't just take a picture straight out of a camera and look at the result. The idea came from a little girl, the daughter of Edwin Land, the inventor of the Polaroid camera, who wanted to see some pictures they'd just taken.

So don't worry if you aren't an expert, or someone else isn't an expert. Your ideas are still worthwhile. More of them might be impossible to use to begin with, because you don't know what is practical, but good ideas don't have to start out practical. It's much easier to take an exciting, inspiring but impractical idea and make it possible to use than it is to take a dull but practical idea and give it appeal.

I'm scared

Related to the way you block your own ideas is the whole area of being frightened or embarrassed of saying anything. Will you get into trouble because you are stirring things up? If it's a different sort of idea, or an idea to change how things are done, someone else might not like it; most change, however sensible, results in resistance. Or will other people just laugh at you for being so stupid? Anyone coming up with a really different idea faces this kind of response, and you should be on the lookout not just for when you feel like this, but to help out others who are clearly embarrassed by their own creativity.

If you're talking about something and someone says, 'I know it's stupid, but couldn't we . . .' or 'I guess it's a dumb idea, but . . .', help them out. Because of the 'I'm not creative' effect, they are trying to shoot down their own idea. They actually tell you it's rubbish as they describe it. That's really helpful. They want to protect themselves in case everyone else is going to laugh at them or worse. Reassure them. After all, if they don't believe in their own ideas, who will? Lots of ideas are stupid – but one of the best ways of getting to *great* ideas is to produce plenty. Most will be ignored. So what? And pretty well every truly great idea sounds dumb at first. Remember those green shoots. Get some confidence, and help others get it too.

Touch of wow!

So let's get on to creativity techniques. They're not magic. They aren't going to have ideas for you while you sit back and watch your favourite TV show. But what they will do is add a touch of 'wow!'. If you just sit down and try to dream up an idea, you've got problems. It could take a while – a very long while. And it's entirely possible that the idea you come up with will be restricted by all the baggage you carry around: how you do things, what you think is possible, and so on.

The techniques give your brain a kick to get it started in a different way. They encourage you to be more exciting. To be more original.

Take a hike

This first technique is hardly a technique at all, but don't ignore it; it can work very well. Think a little bit about what you are trying to achieve. What problem are you trying to solve? What new idea do you need? What kind of creative work do you want to do? Then go out for a 10- to 15-minute walk. Alone – no friends, no iPod, no pager, no cellphone, no personal digital assistant (PDA). Nothing to disturb you but the environment. When you are on your walk, don't consciously look for a solution, but do let the context – what the problem is all about or what the idea is for – flow through your mind in an undirected way.

By the time you come back, you may well have a good idea. This is a more concentrated version of the older technique of just leaving a problem overnight and seeing what you come up with in the morning (this still often works, but it's a bit slow these days). Although it seems as though you aren't doing much, in fact you are playing to your brain's strengths. It isn't very good at coming up with new connections if you are forcing it to give a solution; under pressure it tends to use well-trodden paths. So by just letting the problem drift through your mind, you let the mental processes flow freely and find new possibilities.

Second, by getting out, going for a walk and switching off your mobile technology you get rid of the wrong sort of distractions. Talking to people, checking your schedule, even listening to music, can limit your ability to go to new places in your mind. (This isn't always true of music, as we'll see later, but it's best for this exercise to stay without it even if you work well to music.) And finally you get some more of the right kind of distractions. Unconsciously, as you walk, your senses are taking in data from all around you. These act as little trigger points for thinking differently. But because you aren't really thinking about them, they don't fix the patterns in your brain enough to stop new ideas forming.

This is one of those techniques that gets better and better over time. The reason your ability to come up with ideas like this gets stronger is partly because it helps to have tried other techniques and to have got into the habit of thinking freely, which you will do as you get more into creativity. The technique also works better because the more experiences you have, the more your brain can make strange new connections from a fragment of memory here, a half-seen object there. So don't worry if taking a walk doesn't work every time to begin with.

Even if it doesn't, try it out now and again, and you'll find before long that it's a winner.

Random Picture

Going for a walk is a very subtle technique. This next one is more in your face – but none the worse for that. It's about the best single technique to use to reliably come up with great new ideas. I once used this technique in a course I repeated 40 times with different groups of people. I used the same picture (as you'll see in a moment, a picture is rather important) on the same problem every time. And every single group came up with new ideas I hadn't heard before. Every time.

Aside: Groups and you

I mentioned that I'd done this technique with a group. Pretty well all the techniques in this chapter except going for a walk can be used in a group or individually – so if you're working on a team project they're great for that too. But mostly we're going to concentrate on you in this book. After all, what's more important?

Let's start with that picture. This technique works by using a picture to kick your brain into new ways of thinking – stimulating you to come up with ideas you wouldn't otherwise produce.

The best thing with creativity techniques is to see them in action. I'll give you an example of how to use the Random Picture technique before you have a go yourself. The problem I've set myself is how to make money out of the internet. Everyone else seems to be able to; why not me? Let's use the technique to help with some ideas.

I start, as you may well have guessed from the heading, with a picture, chosen at random. Well, random-ish. First, pick a picture at random. One good way is to pick an interesting-sounding word and use this as the search term in Google images (go to www.google. com and click on Images). Then come up with any image search on Google. (To come up with a word, look out of the window and use the first thing you see, or choose the seventh noun on a randomly selected book page, or just use the first word that comes to mind.) When you've done an image search on that word, pick (say) the fifth image that comes up. Decide what the number is before you search, otherwise it's cheating!

Now the 'random-ish' bit. There are two reasons to dump the picture you've selected and start again. One is if it's something to do with your problem or with the kind of idea you are trying to have. This technique works by breaking you out of your usual way of seeing things. If, say, you were doing a project on supermarkets and wanted to design a whole new way of checking out, then you don't want a picture of a regular supermarket checkout. The other reason for discarding an image is if the picture is practically empty. You want a reasonably rich picture with a fair amount of content. But otherwise stick with it. Don't change it because it looks difficult. The odd ones are often the best.

Let's say I've done this exercise, and I chose the picture opposite at random. For the first stage of the technique I forget all about my problem, or the idea I'm looking for, and just look at the photograph. What does it make me think of? What does it remind me of? I jot down all the associations – the things the photograph makes me think of. They might be personal things – memories, special events – or general things that anyone could think of.

When I looked at this picture I thought of:

- Boats
- Being high up
- Feeling sick
- Queuing
- Fun
- Bare arms
- Screaming

. . . and about 20 other things. With a bit of practice it becomes easy to do this. You might struggle at first, but look at the whole picture and bits of detail, let your mind wander – jot down the things the photograph makes you think of.

Now the picture has done its job and I can put it aside and come back to the problem I was dealing with – in this case, how to make money out of the internet. For the final part of the technique I look at each of the associations in the list and jot down anything it suggests as a solution to my problem or a new idea. What does the word or

phrase make me think of as a way of dealing with my problem? How can I use whatever it is as a starting point?

Let's give that a go. Here's my list again, and I've jotted down the ideas that came to me for how to make money out of the internet. As I noted them down, the ideas are quite short, but I knew what I meant. Bear with me, I'll explain them in a moment.

- **Boats** – boat hire like car hire on city rivers.
- **Being high up** – charge a small amount to steer a webcam on a high building, with an attached water gun (this actually doesn't have to be on a high building).
- **Feeling sick** – 'what medicine is safe with what' guide.
- **Queuing** – phone-based theme park queue length guide.
- **Fun** – nothing.
- **Bare arms** – design your own temporary tattoos online and get them through the mail; send a picture of your skin and we'll send bespoke sun screen.
- **Screaming** – celebrity online auctions.

Take a look at what has come up. The first was inspired by the boat in the picture. We all know how car hire works. You pick up a car, use it then return it (not necessarily to the same place, but to the same company). Why not offer a similar online boat hire service for big cities where the roads are too congested? OK, it's not exactly the sort of business you can start up in your garage, but it's an idea for making money.

The second idea is one of my favourites, and shows you just how this technique should be used. I thought of being high up, as though I was on the swing boat in the picture. That led me on to the idea of being on top of high buildings and putting a webcam there that you can steer by remote control. That would be quite fun and people might pay for it. Pocket money prices for a minute or two in control of the camera. But it would be even better if they could interact with the location, so I imagined fixing a water gun to the camera so that people could find a target and squirt it. The final realization was that with this extra feature the camera didn't need to be up high. The main thing is to site steerable water guns with attached cameras around various locations. You pay money to steer them and squirt people. Excellent. Would you pay a small fee to do this? I know a lot of people would.

Third in my list is a guide to what medicine is safe to take with another prescription. Is it OK to use a painkiller when you are already taking medicine for your hay fever? I don't know. It would be great to have somewhere to check. Of course you would have to be very careful to get your facts right – but to worry about that at this stage is back to trampling on little green shoots. For the moment we just want the ideas; the detail comes later.

The next association I had was queuing. This one is the only idea that's directly about theme parks. Just because the picture is of a theme park, that doesn't mean your ideas have to be about theme parks. But anyone who has been to a big theme park knows you spend ages wandering through the park to get to a ride that you fancy, only to find there's a three-hour queue waiting for you. I'd love a service that told me on my cell phone, using a mobile web browser or by text messages, what the queue lengths were, so I could hurry over to Space Mountain when there was suddenly a 10-minute queue.

I didn't put anything against the heading 'fun'. That was on purpose. Not because I can't think of anything that is fun, but because you don't *have* to come up with something every time. Try each of your associations, but don't worry if nothing comes to mind. In some cases you'll have more than one idea – as with the next association, bare arms. It would be quite simple these days to let people design their own temporary tattoos online, then print them and ship them out. They could even upload photos to become tattoos. Equally, it would be interesting to provide sunscreen to match people's skins. Both ideas from the same association.

Screaming made me think of old TV footage of the Beatles being screamed at by fans, which led me on to celebrities. People are so obsessed with celebrities – why not have a dedicated online auction site that only sells everything and anything that has been touched by, used by or has something to do with celebrities. (If you are thinking, 'it's been done already', remember the little green shoots.)

These aren't all great ideas, but there are some good ones – and I'm sure you would have many more. As I've tried to emphasize, always remember at this stage that the ideas are not fully formed. You'll need to encourage them to grow before you find what's wrong with them. All of them could be improved. You saw that starting to happen with the 'being high up' idea, which went from the rather dull webcams to the much more interesting camera plus water gun. If this happens while you are having the idea, great. Otherwise, put your thoughts to one side, come back a little later and specifically look for ways to make them better and more exciting. Don't worry about making them practical yet. If you have a really great idea you will find a way to make it work.

(A quick aside for you to consider if you are the sort of person who can't help worrying about the failings in an idea once they've heard it. A few people I've mentioned the webcam and water gun idea to have pointed out that I'd be sued. So I need to grow the idea a bit more. One possibility is that I could make sure the water guns were sited at places where people expect to get wet anyway. For example, I could site them on theme park water rides and in fountains that squirt people. If the idea is good enough, you'll find a way to make it work. But don't worry about these for the moment – it's just an example.)

Now it's time for you to have a go yourself. Think of a problem, or a need for an idea. It could be for school work, or in your home life, or to help with some sort of business. Once you've got a problem, find yourself a photograph on Google. Then go through the same process:

- Jot down associations from the photograph.
- Put the photograph aside and go back to your problem.
- Look at each association from the photograph and jot down anything it makes you think of that could help with the problem.

Aside: Why it's essential to write things down

Your brain is utterly brilliant, but one thing it isn't very good at it is juggling a whole pile of things at the same time. You can only handle around seven items in short-term memory at any one time. If you try to remember your ideas instead of jotting them down, they will quickly slip your mind, because you won't have time to get them into the longer-term memory that can handle vast quantities of material. (See Chapter 5 for more on memory.) Always write things down immediately in a creativity exercise. That way, nothing gets lost, and you free up memory to handle the next idea.

Do it now, please, try out the random picture technique for real before you read on. Don't think, 'OK, I'll come back to it later and do it then.' If you don't do it now, you won't do it at all. If you haven't time to do it now, put the book aside and come back to it when you have. If you can't think of a reason for coming up with an idea, use an artificial one, just for the exercise. Come up with a great new product or service that a bank could offer.

Have you really completed the exercise? I don't want to nag, but the *only* way to get value out of these creativity techniques is to try them out. It's not enough just to read about them. So, if you have used a random picture, congratulations, keep it up. If you haven't, please, trust me, it's important you don't go any further until you have had a go.

Attributes

The picture technique we just used is great for coming up with something completely different. It's likely to produce a bunch of really new ideas, not connected to anything you do at the moment. But that's not always what you need. It may be that you want to improve on something that already exists without going in a whole new direction. If that is what you are looking for, this could be the technique for you.

To use the attributes technique, first note down what is important about your problem area, or the area in which you are trying to get an idea. What are its attributes – what makes it what it is, makes it different from something else? Once you've got those attributes you can start to play around with them, to change them, to make them into something different and more interesting.

Let's say you've got a technology assignment to design a totally new kind of toothbrush – but it still has to be a functioning toothbrush. So to use this technique you sit down and list out the attributes of a toothbrush. What's a toothbrush like? What's it made of? What makes it a toothbrush as opposed to a hairbrush, or a walking stick? You might get a list a bit like this:

- Handle
- Bristles
- Plastic
- Cheap
- Electric
- Rotating head
- Different sizes of bristle
- Light
- Has to be replaced
- Fits in your mouth

. . . and I'm sure you can think of more. Now we go back to those attributes and see what we can do by varying one or more of them.

Let's say you chose 'handle' to vary first. What would a toothbrush be like if it didn't have a handle? Spend a minute thinking about that, jotting down ideas. You might come up with something like this:

- Chewable toothbrush
- Toothbrush that fits on your finger
- Toothbrush fixed to the wall like a hand dryer
- Without a handle, you could see what you were doing better
- Toothbrush that runs around in your mouth like an automated pool cleaner
- Living toothbrush
- Drinkable toothbrush

. . . and so on. A fair number of these exist already. 'Chewable' could be either gum that claims to reduce plaque, or the chewable tooth-brushes you buy from a dispenser in a little plastic sphere – but you could make it something different. A toothbrush that fits on your finger could be one of the tooth cleaning pads you can already buy, but also could be more like a toothbrush, but one that clips on a finger end, as your flexible finger can reach into places that a handle can't. Note the item near the middle of the list 'without a handle, you could see what you were doing better'. This isn't a specific variation, but is a starting point you could use to inspire an idea. Starting from this, instead of worrying about not having a handle, you could think, 'How could I design a toothbrush so the user can see what they are doing better?'

There are lots of ideas there from just one attribute. You could go on to get many more from the other attributes, or even from combining attributes. Be prepared, if your mind takes a flight of fancy, to follow it. Don't feel you have to stick rigidly to the rules. For instance, when I saw the word 'light' (meaning that toothbrushes are usually light), it made me think of a toothbrush *made of* light, or a toothbrush with a light on it so I could see where I was cleaning in the dark recesses of the mouth, which was quite different from the way the attribute is normally used, but is equally worth exploring.

Have a go yourself. Either produce your own attributes for a new toothbrush, or try a totally different exercise using attributes. This technique works very well when you are looking at something real and solid, though it can be used just as effectively on other things – for example when looking for a new way to approach a traditional story form.

Aside: The rules

Creativity techniques don't really have rules. They are a set of guidelines, suggestions on how to free up your mind. But if you find an idea coming up that doesn't fit with 'the rules', don't worry, grab it! Rules is often another word for unnecessary assumptions, at least as far as ideas go. You can always put the rules back after you've got the idea – but that's just a matter of making the idea practical, and it's much easier to make a great idea that breaks the rules practical than to take a dull idea that obeys all the rules and make it appealing.

For instance, if you wanted to use this technique to write a horror story, you could start by noting down the key attributes of a traditional horror story and varying it. That way you would come up with something new and original. This is a technique that was used very successfully in the horror/action/comedy TV show *Buffy the Vampire Slayer*. The writers would consciously look for the traditional attributes of a piece of action in a horror movie, then would change what happened away from the expected. This is obvious even in creator Joss Whedon's central premise. In a normal horror story the young girl is the prey of the evil creature. Here, Buffy is the predator, and the vampires are the targets.

Reversal

The reversal technique is a way of thinking up new ideas that goes all the way back to the 1950s. It was one of the very first to be used, and it's still pretty good today. The idea is to find something that's absolutely central to the problem you are working on, and instead of taking the expected direction, you reverse it. This makes it particularly good when the situation you are dealing with involves movement or a connection of some sort.

So, for example, if your problem was how to make a car go faster, you could list as many ways as you can think of to make a car go more slowly. Or if you wanted to make communication better in your school or university, then you would first think of as many ways as you can to make communication worse.

Imagine I'd written out a nice big list of ways to make it hard to communicate. I can then use these methods in three different ways to come up with new ideas. The first is just to reverse them. For example, if I'd said, 'don't have a PA system', then I could turn that round to 'have a PA system'. But this tends to be a weak way to come up with ideas, because you normally think of the negative by reversing a positive – you probably started from the idea of a PA system, so there's nothing new.

A second, and better, way to make use of the reversal is to actually do the reversal, but in a special or limited way. For instance, you might say 'ban mobile phones (cellphones)' as a way of reducing communication. But if you say 'ban mobile phones in class', or 'no mobile phones in lectures', then you will improve the communication in the room at that time.

A third option is to use the negative as the inspiration for something quite different. For example, one of the ways you might suggest to make it harder to communicate could be 'put paper bags over everyone's head'. This doesn't sound too good (though it's better than plastic bags). But that might make you think of 'put a name badge round everyone's neck' so you know who everyone is. Or you might think of everyone being issued with a bag they wear that's their personal mailbox, so people can slip notes in it throughout the day. Or the paper bag could become a special piece of blogging paper; everyone is expected to make one note – ideas for changing how things are done in your college, or a commentary on school life, or whatever – and stick it up on special blogging noticeboards. (To make sure everyone contributes, your blogging paper could have a special code on it that identifies it as yours, and if that code appears on the noticeboard, you could get some kind of reward.) And I'm sure you could think of more and better ideas just inspired by that one 'paper bag over the head' thought.

Another, related technique that might work better in situations where things are less directional, situations where it's not so obvious what reversing means, is to identify something that is central to the situation and take it out. For example, if you wanted to improve a restaurant business, or start a new and different restaurant, you might ask, 'How could we run a successful restaurant without providing any food?' or 'How could we have a successful restaurant with no tables and chairs or no cutlery?' Or if you were trying to improve a school, 'How could we have a successful school with no teachers, or with no buildings?'

As with the reversal, you could take the ideas that come up in response literally, or you could modify them to keep the originality but make them more interesting or easier to do. Try out the technique now, before moving on.

Being someone else

Creativity is all about seeing things differently, so you can make new connections that you wouldn't otherwise have thought of. One way to see something differently is to see it through someone else's eyes. You might literally ask someone else what they think, but there's a creativity technique you can use that involves getting yourself into someone else's way of looking at things.

To start with, you need to pick a person. It could be a real-life person, or a fictional character, or just a general type of person. Try to pick a character who is as far as possible from your own way of looking at things, and whom you wouldn't normally associate with the problem. If this isn't easy, you can pick a person at random from the list below. Use a watch's second hand/indicator to come up a number between 1 and 60 first. Here's the list:

1 Marilyn Monroe
2 Queen Elizabeth I of England
3 A casino croupier
4 Adolf Hitler
5 Attila the Hun
6 A librarian
7 William Shakespeare
8 Macbeth
9 A Roman centurion
10 A plumber
11 Dr Livingstone
12 David Beckham
13 Eyore (from Winnie the Pooh)
14 The current US president
15 A pet rabbit
16 A mass murderer
17 A prison warder
18 John Wayne
19 The Lone Ranger

20   Robin Hood
21   A computer programmer
22   Snoopy
23   Ludwig van Beethoven
24   Karl Marx
25   Groucho Marx
26   Niccolò Machiavelli
27   The Prime Minister of the UK
28   George Washington
29   A nasturtium
30   A surgeon
31   The head teacher of a large inner-city school
32   A circus clown
33   A circus trapeze artist
34   A poet
35   A Roman Catholic priest
36   A rabbi
37   Confucius
38   Frank Lloyd Wright
39   Sherlock Holmes
40   Hercule Poirot
41   A Martian
42   Winston Churchill
43   Count Dracula
44   Mao Tse-tung
45   Billy the Kid
46   Tutankhamun
47   Charles Darwin
48   An ant
49   A court jester
50   Orville Wright
51   Paul McCartney
52   Neil Armstrong
53   A blind person
54   A deaf person
55   Mr Spock
56   Donald Duck
57   A New York cab driver
58   The Pope
59   Superman
60   A beggar in Bombay

Your only excuse for changing your selection is if you don't have the faintest idea who this character is.

Spend a minute or two thinking about your chosen person. Don't worry if you don't know too much about them, just imagine what they're like. Then imagine that they have to come up with an idea for you, or solve your problem. What would they do? How would they see things?

Write down a list of ideas from your character – make sure they come up with at least five or six. Now look through them. Some you might be able to use directly. Others might suggest something more connected to the real world that you wouldn't already have thought of.

Like all the techniques I've put in this book, you can use this one on your own or with other people. This is one that works particularly well with other people. Each of you takes a different character. Think of your ideas separately in the role of your character, then go through them one at a time, explaining them. The rest of the group should take those ideas as they are suggested and work with them, changing them into even better ideas. (When doing this, you don't need to stay in character, but you can if you like.)

This technique is often used for problem solving, because the character will have a very different viewpoint. This is where it can really help to get someone as far away from the problem as possible. I've seen Queen Elizabeth I come up with some great ideas for new ways of selling TVs, because she didn't really understand what a TV was (come on, she was born in 1533, what do you expect?). She thought it was for looking at people at a distance, a sort of remote telescope, which led to some very useful confusion.

The 'being someone else' technique doesn't just have to be about problem solving, though. If you are stuck for ideas for a creative essay or story, you can always get help from one of these characters. You might imagine what your essay would be like if it were written by one of these characters. You could even make it a story narrated by one of the characters. To illustrate how this is possible even with the hardest character of the bunch, on page 141 you will find a short story called 'Observations' narrated by a nasturtium plant.

Getting a boost

Being creative is hard work – more so in some ways than running round a track or digging a hole in the ground. It's not something you can do hour after hour without losing energy. I always think it's as though your creativity gradually sinks into your bottom as you sit trying to think. After a while, you need to do something about it. I've looked elsewhere (see page 121) at splitting your work into chunks and taking breaks, but there are other things you can do to give your creativity a boost.

In the short term (unless you are diabetic) a shot of sugar – a chocolate bar, a non-diet soda or a cookie/biscuit – can give you a little jolt of energy, though it's not something I would recommend too often, for obvious reasons. Just getting out of your chair and taking a walk around outside for a couple of minutes can help too. Or alternatively you can take action to get your brain into a different gear.

You can do this by spending a couple of minutes randomly browsing the web, for example. A great way to do this is to use StumbleUpon, which is a little toolbar that sits at the top of your web browser and takes you from site to site. Initially these sites are random, but as you register what you like and what you don't, you should find you hit more and more sites that you find inspiring. (See www.stumble upon.com for details.) Alternatively, read a short story, or listen to a new piece of music. In either case, limit your time strictly to between two and five minutes. These are activities that can easily eat up your time if you let them take over. (One thing I do to stop StumbleUpon taking over is to have two web browsers installed on my computer, Internet Explorer and Firefox. I have Stumbleupon installed in the browser I don't use as often, so I'm less tempted!)

Taking off the wheel nuts

There's an old saying that you often used to find stuck up as a poster on office walls: 'When you're up to your neck in alligators, there's no time to drain the swamp.' Often, busy people (or just lazy people) say they haven't got time to think about being creative or to use one of these techniques or whatever.

They're idiots.

If you think that's harsh, imagine this. You're driving along and you see someone broken down at the side of the road. You stop to help. (If this is unlikely to happen, imagine it's a very attractive someone of the opposite sex.) When you get closer, you realize this person has a flat tyre. He or she is bent over the wheel, trying to take off the wheel nuts with bare hands.

You don't understand. 'Why are you doing that?' you say. 'Why don't you just go round to the back of the car and get the wrench? That way you'll get the nuts off easily.' The stranded person looks at you with a wild look in his or her eye. 'I can't. I'm in a hurry. I just don't have time to go and get the wrench.' So there they stay, trying to get the wheel nuts off with their bare hands.

Of course that's just a story. No one would do that for real. Yet that's exactly what happens when you say, 'I haven't got time to use a creativity technique.' Or even 'I haven't got time to think.'

By taking that extra minute or two, stepping back from the problem and thinking about how to do it, maybe using a quick technique, you are doing the equivalent of getting the wrench out of the car, instead of using your bare hands. You are getting the right tool for the job. And that can't be a bad thing.

More techniques and free software

I've only room to include a few techniques here, but there are hundreds of ways to stimulate new ideas out there. See the Appendix for suggestions of books to read. You'll also find more techniques on websites like my own, www.cul.co.uk; go to the Information Site and take a look around. It's particularly worth taking a look at the software section, which includes details of some free software you can use to help have ideas, or to structure your thoughts.

Giving the brain a workout

The techniques we've looked at so far are designed to crack specific requirements. You want an idea – they help you get one. You want to fix a problem – they help you work out how to do it. But they also have the effect of helping your brain get better at being creative. Creativity is all about making new connections, and there is good evidence that the more you practise doing this, the easier it becomes. So before we leave the world of creativity techniques, it's important to take a look at techniques that aren't there to solve a particular problem, but are particularly aimed at exercising your brain and making it more effective at coming up with great ideas.

Puzzles, problems and mind stretching

It is widely accepted (though I am not sure how much research has been done into this) that doing puzzles, working on logic problems and things of this kind can help you be more creative. I say this reluctantly through gritted teeth, because I hate doing puzzles, particularly the physical kind. Rubik's cube brings out a strong urge in me to peel off the stickers and put them back on a matching face. My preferred technique when solving puzzles involving bits of bent wire is to use a pair of pliers. But if you can bring yourself to do them (or, even better, if you enjoy them), these things seem to help.

Before I give you some specific mind-stretching exercises, though, you need to be aware of the dwarf in an elevator pitfall. This shows how taking the traditional approach to puzzles and logic problems can lead to your being less creative, not more. There's a well-known type of logic problem called a lateral thinking problem. With problems like this, you are told a little story and have to work out what's going on. You make suggestions until you come up with the right answer, and that's where things go very wrong for creativity.

Aside: Lateral thinking

Lateral thinking is a term dreamed up by the psychologist Edward de Bono in the 1960s. The idea is that you come at the problem from a different direction, rather than the obvious one. De Bono has written a huge amount about creativity, but don't worry if you find his books hard going; there are many books on the subject that are easier to read.

Here's a popular lateral thinking problem. Every morning, a man gets into a lift on the 23rd floor of the block of flats where he lives and rides down to the ground floor. When he comes back to the building, he gets into the lift, rides up to the 16th floor, then walks the rest of the way to the 23rd. Why does he do this?

After coming up with various suggestions, you are supposed to realize eventually that the man is a dwarf. He has no problem pressing the button for the ground floor, which is near the bottom of the control panel, but he can only reach up as far as the 16th floor button; the button for the 23rd floor is too high. There's nothing wrong with this answer, but to say that this is the 'right answer' totally misses the point of creativity and lateral thinking. Pretty well any problem out there in the real world (as opposed to in the artificial world of a test or puzzle) has lots of right answers. In this particular case, for example, all of these are perfectly good answers:

- He needs some exercise – but not too much exercise.
- There is a shop or café on the 16th floor where he stops off on the way home.
- All the buttons above 16 have been vandalized and don't work.
- His girlfriend lives on the 16th floor.
- He is superstitious and 16 is his lucky number.

. . . and so on. I should think you could think up another half-dozen answers in just a minute. (Try it before reading on.) And they are all just as good as the original 'right' answer. So by all means try out lateral thinking problems as part of your work out for your brain, but don't limit yourself to a single answer.

Now let's try out a few of those puzzles. You don't have to do them all now – perhaps do one or two, and make a note to come back to the rest when you are working on your creativity. But what's really important is that once you start one you actually try it. Don't just read it, skip to the solution and say 'hmm'. You won't get any benefit if you don't try it first.

After the mind-stretching puzzles there are a number of rather different exercises that I've called mental workouts. These are less frustrating if you don't like puzzles, and more oriented to getting specific aspects of your mind working better. Again, you don't need to do them all straight away, but check them all out now and make a note to come back and do them later.

In the Appendix there are suggestions on where to find more puzzles, both in books and the physical variety.

Mind Stretch 1: Get the sandwich

Some lateral thinking puzzles specifically require you to look at things in a different or unusual way. This first mind-stretching exercise is a little more gentle. It can be solved with pure logic – but the answer isn't necessarily obvious.

Every day I go down at lunchtime (which can be any time randomly between 12 noon and 1 p.m.) to the local metro station and stand between the platforms for the uptown and downtown trains. Both uptown and downtown trains come every ten minutes. I catch whichever train comes first, travel one stop and get off. Then I go to the nearest sandwich shop to buy lunch. Somehow, though, I almost always go to *The Savoury Sub* (the shop near the station in the uptown direction) rather than *The Beautiful Baguette* (the shop near the station in the downtown direction). In fact, I've noticed that, on average, I only go *The Beautiful Baguette* once every two weeks. Why is this?

If you haven't already got an answer, don't read any further until you get one. Go back, read it through again and think. If necessary, put the book down and think about it. Take a little walk, then come back to it.

I'm trusting you here. To read on any further, you should have an answer.

Both uptown and downtown trains run every ten minutes. As it happens, the uptown trains arrive at the station one minute before the downtown trains. Because of this, there is only one minute out of every ten when the next train is the downtown one. So I catch the uptown train, on average, once every ten tries, or once every two working weeks.

As I said, this is a straightforward (if slightly puzzling) logic problem. It has a clear, simple answer. Sometimes this happens. But remember there are many real-world problems that have a lot of different answers. And even this might have another answer. If you came up with a different answer to the puzzle, one that makes just as much sense, pat yourself on the back.

Mind Stretch 2: Three in quick succession

The second of our ventures into giving your brain a kicking to get it working involves three very short puzzles. Don't spend too long on them; try to get through them as quickly as you can.

Here we go:

1   What is the result of adding 15 and 5 three times?
2   A farmer was infuriated to see five rabbits eating his lettuces. He shot one rabbit – how many rabbits were left?
3   Is there any way to drop a hard-boiled egg onto a very delicate balsa-wood toy from the top of a skyscraper without damaging it?

As before, please don't read the solution and discussion below without trying out the puzzles. It only takes a few seconds. If you are cheating, please go back and try them. As there are three answers, you might like to note them down somewhere so you aren't trying to remember what the answers were.

Final check. Have you got three answers?

My answers are as follows:

1   Twenty (it doesn't matter how many times you add 15 and 5, you still get 20).
2   No rabbits (the other four ran away).
3   Yes, there is a way to drop a hard-boiled egg on to a very delicate balsa-wood toy from the top of a skyscraper without damaging it (it's actually very hard to crack a skyscraper by dropping an egg from it).

Each of these puzzles works by providing an answer that is different from the expected one. Just like a creativity technique, the world is seen in a different way. Once you've groaned at the answers (if you hadn't already guessed them), take a minute to examine what was happening.

In each case, you knew the answer. If you came up with something different, you just didn't understand the question. And that can often be a difficulty when you are trying to be creative. You can end up solving the wrong problem, coming up with an idea that doesn't do what the person who came up with the question intended.

In all cases it is the wording of the problem that tends to make people go wrong. The wording is accurate, but ambiguous. In number 3, for example, there are three nouns that 'it' could refer to: the egg, the toy and the skyscraper. The convention of the English language is that it's the last one mentioned that 'it' should link to, in this case the skyscraper. But the natural inclination is to think of breaking the egg or the toy, rather than the skyscraper, because these are things we associate with breakages.

In the middle puzzle the ambiguity is a little more subtle. The problem here is that we don't know what is meant by 'left' in 'how many rabbits were left'. If it means 'left in the lettuce patch', then the answer certainly is none. If it were 'how many were left in existence of the original five', then it's four. And if it's 'how many rabbits are left in existence in the world', we are probably talking billions.

You might think I've forgotten my line about most problems having more than one acceptable solution. If you had different answers, what was wrong with yours? Probably nothing. But whereas in a real-life problem-solving exercise the aim is to solve the problem, so any of the solutions would do, here you are trying to exercise your mental muscles, so it's important to see what the intended answer was. Practising doing this sort of problem helps you get better at being ready for the unexpected twist that life can sometimes throw at you.

Mind Stretch 3: The magic mix

I have two bottles, one with water in it, the other containing wine. I pour a measure of wine into the water bottle (there is enough space in the bottle to do this without it overflowing). I then pour an equal measure from the water bottle back into the wine bottle. At the end, there is just as much water in the wine as there is wine in the water. Which of the following have to be true to make these mixes balance out exactly? (you can choose more than one):

- The bottles are the same size.
- There is the same amount of wine and of water to begin with.
- The contents of the water bottle are thoroughly mixed after the measure of wine is poured into the bottle.
- The contents of the wine bottle are thoroughly mixed after the measure of water and wine is poured back into the bottle.
- The wine has the same density as the water.
- The water and wine mix with each other.

. . . or is it impossible to be certain that there is just as much water in the wine as there is wine in the water, even if all these conditions are true?

As usual, please don't go any further until you've decided which of the conditions have to apply (or whether it's even possible).

Really sure? Just check back over those conditions one more time.

Surprisingly, none of the conditions has to hold true; there will always be just as much wine in the water as there is water in the wine. Think of it like this: at the end of the process, the wine bottle has exactly the same amount of liquid in it as it did to start with. So however much wine was taken out of the bottle, exactly the same amount of water must have been added to it. The same goes in reverse for the water bottle.

As often happens, the way that the question was phrased can distract you from the true facts. Even if you got the right answer, the chances are that the phrasing proved a distraction. You probably worried about whether or not the wine and the water mixed properly, for example. Thinking about what is actually happening, rather than what you are being shown, can be crucial to good creative problem solving.

Mind Stretch 4: The missing bullet

A man stands in the centre of a large field. There are four horses in the field, one at each corner: a bay horse, a chestnut horse, a white horse and a black horse. For reasons we needn't go into, the man has to kill his horses. (No animals will be harmed in the working of this puzzle.) If the man must remain at the centre of the field, the horses stay at the four corners and he is a perfect shot, how can he make sure that none of his horses remains alive, using only three bullets?

This is a puzzle that might take a couple of read-throughs before you can come up with any ideas. Don't rush it.

Please do make some attempt at a solution before reading on.

One possibility is that only three of the four horses belong to the man, so he only needs to shoot three to make sure that 'none of his horses' remains alive. A second possibility is that one of the horses was already dead of the terrible and painful disease that was about to claim the lives of the others – hence his need to shoot them. With only three horses alive to begin with, he only needs three bullets. A third possibility is that the white horse was a chalk carving or a picture of a horse and so had never been alive. There are more solutions too.

As with the dwarf in the lift, there are plenty of right answers here, and the importance is not coming up with 'the' right answer, but seeing how there are many possible answers. Before going on, go back and see if you can come up with at least one more answer, as different as possible from the others.

If you can't shake off your love of 'the right answer', you might be wondering what the real right answer is in this case, just as some people will tell you that the dwarf was the right answer in the elevator example. If so, you've really missed the point. It doesn't matter in any way what 'the right answer' is. In this particular example I can't even give you a single answer, because this puzzle was specifically dreamed up to illustrate multiple right answers. It doesn't have any single answer that is the original right one.

Mind Stretch 5: A girdle round about the earth

In Shakespeare's *A Midsummer Night's Dream*, Puck says, 'I'll put a girdle round about the earth in forty minutes.' (Yes, we have creativity and culture too.) For this mind-stretching exercise, I'd like you to take rather less than 40 minutes: try not to spend more than two minutes on it.

Imagine you had a very long rope with no stretch in it. This rope is just the right length to go all the way round the world – that's around 40,000 kilometres. Now imagine we added 3 metres to the length of the rope, and managed to lift it evenly off the surface of the planet to take up the slack.

Guess what size of gap would be formed between the rope and the surface of the earth. Even if you are great at geometry, don't try to work it out, just guess. Then take an extra couple of minutes to think about how you would work out exactly how far the rope would be from the earth, but again there's no need to work out the answer.

If you haven't already done the two parts of the problem, please do them now. Don't read any further until you have. Remember, just a quick guess first, then think how you would work out an exact value, but you don't need to actually do the working out.

Got an answer? Then read on.

The guess is usually that the rope lifts a tiny distance off the surface – perhaps a millimetre or less – because just 3 metres has been added to a rope that was 40,000 kilometres long. That's very little change, so presumably it means very little change in the distance the rope is from the surface.

Unfortunately, circles don't work like that. The circumference of the circle – the length of the rope in this case – is always $2\pi r$. Pi (π) is about 3, so that makes the length of the rope roughly six times the radius of the circle it makes around the Earth. So, the radius was around $C/6$, where C is the circumference. Now we add 3 to the circumference, making it $C + 3$. So the radius becomes $(C + 3)/6$ – or $C/6 + 3/6$. In other words, the radius has increased by roughly $3/6$, about half a metre. Much bigger than you might expect.

Our instinctive reaction to a problem is based on feeling and common sense. Sometimes this is very valuable. Complex or fuzzy problems are often impossible to analyse in detail, and getting a gut feel for something can sometimes be the only way to decide what to do (at least in a reasonable timescale). But you've got to remember that common sense can often lead you astray. Be prepared to challenge what seems obvious. Don't just take your intuition for granted; test it, and get to the ways it lets you down.

Here's just one example where intuition gets it wrong. Imagine you are watching a big lottery being drawn; someone is going to be made a millionaire. Six numbers are drawn from a possible 49. Out the numbers come, one after another: 24 – 39 – 6 – 41 – 17 – 29. Most people sigh, tear up their slips and forget about it. It's no big deal, it happens every week. But now imagine the same scene with a very different outcome. Let's pick up the commentary. 'They're using the machine they call Delilah for the draw tonight, started by none other than a former member of Blondie. Here comes the first number and . . . what are the chances of that? The first number is 1. OK, next choice, well would you believe it? Two. That's incredible. And the third number's coming through now. Hey, is this a joke? The third number is 3 . . .'

And so it goes on until the draw is complete: 1 – 2 – 3 – 4 – 5 – 6. All neatly in sequence. There is an uproar. The pay-out is suspended while the draw machine is investigated. Questions are asked, all the way up to the government. Yet no one can find anything wrong. How could this be? How could such an unlikely result happen?

But here's the strange thing. Both those results, 24 – 39 – 6 – 41 – 17 – 29 and 1 – 2 – 3 – 4 – 5 – 6, have exactly the same chance of winning. *Exactly* the same chance. So why was one just another draw, and the other incredible? Because common sense doesn't understand probability. That's why casinos make a lot of money. If you are ever tempted to buy a lottery ticket, remember you are buying a ticket with the same chance of winning as 1 – 2 – 3 – 4 – 5 – 6. Be very wary when relying on intuition and common sense.

Mind Stretch 6: The great escape

Here's an unusual little problem for you to consider. You are locked in a cell. (I don't know why you should be locked in a cell. Maybe you do.) The cell has a circular floor 5 metres in diameter, and smooth concrete walls 4 metres high. In the centre of the floor is a hole, 10 centimetres deep. At the bottom of the hole is a smooth wooden ball which drops easily into the hole, but is only a little smaller in diameter than the hole itself. You have been stripped naked and have nothing about your person. You are given three conventional wire paperclips. You will only be allowed out of the cell if you can get the ball out of the hole. What do you do?

If you haven't got a solution, keep trying for a little longer.

Do I really need to send you back by now? Surely you know not to read any further until you have got an answer?

There's a natural tendency to assume that since you are given only one tool, there must be some way of using that tool. Unfortunately, this assumption is flawed. Just because you are given something, it doesn't have to be useful, nor do you have to use it. The paperclips aren't really very helpful in this instance. However, you do have a way of getting the ball out of the hole. After all, wooden balls float, so all you have to is get some liquid into the hole. Exactly how you are going to do that is up to you. The rest of the solution is left to your imagination.

Sometimes, trying to use everything you've been given in coming up with a solution to a problem can mess up your solution. This problem demonstrates how it can be useful to drop some of the 'given' input to see what else is available. As with most of these exercises, this is a valuable lesson for being creative in the real world. Sometimes in the artificial world of examinations you might be expected to use all the 'givens' – but you shouldn't have to. If you really had to in this instance, having floated the ball out of the hole you could use the paperclips to pick it up, because you might not want to touch it.

I'm not saying that you should always ignore the tools you're given – that would be stupid – but giving some consideration to how things would work without the materials and tools you've got can be valuable. Try applying this thinking to various everyday problems and situations.

Mind Stretch 7: Three more quickies

Here is another set of three very short puzzles to attempt as quickly as you can. Don't work up a sweat, just get a solution as quickly as you can, note it down, and move on.

1   Which game, with four letters in its name, starts with a T, originated in Scotland and is played outdoors?
2   Pandas are endangered, but they have an aid to survival that is totally unique to their species. What is it?
3   Why were so many great composers German?

Really, really have a go before reading any further. Remember to write those answers down; don't strain your limited short-term memory.

This is the last mind stretch, so make sure you have three answers before reading on.

The answers are:

1 The game with four letters in its name that starts with a T, originated in Scotland and is played outdoors is golf (it starts with a tee).
2 The unique aid to the survival of the panda species is baby pandas.
3 So many great composers are German because they were born in Germany. (If they'd been born somewhere else, they wouldn't be German.)

Each of these twisted little puzzles depends on taking something about the information you are given and using it in a way that you don't expect. Each of the answers given is perfectly logical (OK, the first one is a bit forced), but it isn't the obvious one. When you are trying to come up with an idea, a non-obvious solution can be not only effective but much simpler than the 'obvious' solutions. For example, in puzzle 3, if you didn't go for the very simple reason in my answer, you would have to start going into the cultural and economic influences, or the impact of the German church – all much more complex than the outstandingly simple answer I've provided. It seems a bit of a cheat as an answer, but as long as it does the job, this doesn't matter in the slightest.

One of the essentials in getting a good solution to a problem is making sure that you have fully understood the problem. Pull it apart. Look at each aspect of it separately. For example, in question 1 above, 'with four letters in its name' was quite innocent, but such a statement won't necessarily always be so straightforward. Try this: think of a yellow fruit with three letters in its name. The answer is 'banana'. The three letters are A, B and N.

Mental workout 1: Hiding a secret

The mental workouts that follow are rather different from the mind-stretching exercises. They are much more open-ended. This first one bridges the gap between a puzzle and a true workout. It still has some of the elements of a puzzle, in that we're looking for the solution to a problem, but there are no tricks or special twists here. It's just a stimulation to help you think creatively and get your mental muscles in action.

Imagine you had a small amount of text – enough to fill a normal piece of paper. You are in a small room that contains only a PC, a desk with three drawers, a bookcase and a candle. The bookcase has half a dozen thick reference books on it, and a couple of filing boxes. How would you hide the text in such a way that you could get the text back from its hidden form, yet no one else would be able to get to your secret? To make it more interesting, see if you can think of a way whereby you could put the concealed text on plain view, so anyone could see it without moving anything, but no one would realize they were seeing it. You can use whatever tools you like to turn the text into a readily concealed form, provided the tools can be hidden away too.

Although this isn't a puzzle, it's still worth spending a little time working on it, coming up with some ideas before going on. See if you can come up with two or three different solutions. Don't read the rest of this section until you have some solutions.

I once needed a creative solution to this problem for something I was writing, and, feeling lazy, I asked a hotshot computer programmer what he would do. He suggested using a picture on the PC. Pictures are stored in files which use three numbers to specify the colour of each dot (pixel) that makes up the picture. By using the least important bit of data for each dot, you can store a lot of information without making an obvious difference to the picture. The picture could then be used as a backdrop or screensaver on the computer, keeping the information in plain view. Of course, you would need appropriate software to accomplish this, but that's just a tool. Interestingly, since then a software company has started selling such a piece of software. This isn't the only solution, nor the most creative; it's just one example. Others I can come up with quickly include:

- Mark letters in a book that you leave in plain sight.
- Spell it out in Morse code using pins on a noticeboard (or make the pin pricks and take the pins away, to make it harder to spot).
- Write it in candle wax on a sheet of paper, so it only becomes visible when paint is poured over it.
- If the room has exposed bricks, spell it out in Braille, using indentations in the mortar in place of the usual Braille bumps.

. . . and I'm sure you can think of even better ones.

It might seem that thinking out the answer to such an unlikely problem won't help everyday creativity, but the processes involved are perfect for strengthening the creative ability. The advantage of this type of exercise is that you can think up your own with very little effort. Just put together a near-impossible requirement (anything from a 'locked room' murder mystery to an automatic shoelace tier) and spend a couple of minutes working on solutions.

Mental workout 2: Make it a metaphor

Now we are on to a pure exercise to help your brain work better. There are no right answers.

Use a newspaper (or a web news site) to generate a list of five items. They could be people, places, events, objects – anything, as long as the five are quite different. Now spend no more than a minute on each item, jotting down a series of metaphors. These are just things you can say it's like – with short reasons attached. For example, one of the items in today's news is about New York. I might think New York is like:

- a forest – because it has lots of tall buildings;
- an ant's nest – because of all the people milling around in a small space;
- a jewel – because of all the bright lights and wealth.

. . . and so on.

Don't think too much about your metaphors, just let them flow. Remember, there is genuinely no 'right answer' here. As long as you believe that what you are saying is reasonable, that's fine. If you have real problems getting started, think of the key attributes of whatever you are trying to create a metaphor for, then think of other things with similar attributes. But you should aim to make metaphor formation natural, as it will produce attributes you weren't consciously aware of.

Metaphors are really valuable because they tap into the way the brain stores information. Our 'mental models' of the world are really fancy metaphors. Getting used to making metaphors, to seeing metaphors for whatever it is you are looking at or reading about, is a great way to improve personal creativity. A metaphor can also often be used to solve a problem or generate an idea. By saying that a problem is like something, we can find new approaches. Finally, metaphor is valuable in improving your personal writing skills, useful in a whole swathe of study subjects. Good writers make use of metaphor to put across a concept that's hard to explain in other ways. A metaphor packs a lot of information baggage into very few words.

This is an exercise you could repeat regularly for a while. Perhaps try it weekly for a month, then reinforce it every few months, keeping the metaphorical mental muscles (metaphorical in more than one sense, given that the idea of having mental 'muscles' is itself a metaphor) in trim.

Mental workout 3: It's story time

For this exercise you will need a library or a bookshop. Find a *short* short story (no more than five or six pages). It should be unusual, maybe science fiction or fantasy or just about an extreme circumstance – it shouldn't be everyday. Read the story through. Reading a short story can be more than just entertainment; done the right way, it can enhance your creativity.

Now spend a few minutes thinking about the story. What did the author do and say that was unexpected, or that you don't normally encounter in real life? What sort of point(s) of view does the story use? Try to get below the surface of the story into the mind of the writer.

In putting together a story, the writer suspends reality and looks at life differently. This is essential for creativity. If you are having difficulty finding an appropriate story, see if the library has a copy of my book *Imagination Engineering* (written with Paul Birch). It's a textbook on business creativity, so the main content isn't really important, but each chapter ends with a short story specially chosen for the purpose of stimulating creative thought. If you can't lay your hands on that, read the short story 'Observations' at the back of this book.

I have to stress how important it is to find some unusual fiction. Great literature often portrays very ordinary circumstances. Feel free to read that as well, but this exercise needs something more than ordinary literature can offer: that glimpse of a different world that will inspire a new viewpoint in the reader. Familiarizing yourself with the way a writer suspends reality and devises a fictional world with an alternative viewpoint is excellent preparation for being more creative.

You can get plenty more value by keeping up your fiction reading. If you see reading as part of your lifetime learning, rather than just entertainment, perhaps you will give it a higher priority. A regular diet of unusual fiction will keep your creativity on the bubble.

Mental workout 4: Seeing is beleafing

For this workout you need to get hold of a reasonably broad tree leaf. Find somewhere comfortable and sit down. You are going to be asked to do a number of things with the leaf. Read the first numbered sentence, do it, then come back and take on the next requirement. Try to focus as much as possible on one activity at a time; don't keep them all in your head at once.

1   Look at the leaf in a general way: turn it over in your hand and get a feel for it.
2   Look closely at the leaf. Examine the fine detail. Look at the veins, the edges of the leaf, the way it joins on to the stem, and so on.
3   Think yourself into the leaf. What is under the surface? It doesn't matter if you don't really know; just imagine what goes together to make up the leaf. Pretend you are very tiny and can actually go into the leaf – what would you see?
4   Think from the leaf back to the tree. How would the leaf join on to the tree? What would surround it? How would the light and the air play around it?
5   Finally, gently tear the leaf. Try to feel the individual parts of the leaf resisting your pressure. Look at the torn edge: how does it differ from the natural edges?

Everyone knows that leaves are common and uninspiring – any garden or park is full of the things. Yet they are complex, intriguing objects. Getting back a little of the sort of outlook you might have had when you were six or eight years old is amazingly helpful in being creative. A kid's creativity only works because he or she doesn't know everything; taking a moment to look at a leaf makes it obvious how much all of us usually take for granted. However old you are now, your 'knowing' is very limited indeed.

Take the time to look at other everyday things more closely. You can't do it all the time, but to do it every now and then is a wonderful exercise. It's something you can do if you are stuck on a train or a bus. For a few minutes just stare out of the window and really look at what's around you. Look at a building; really look at it. If you're in a shopping street, look at the buildings above the shop fronts. Most people never even see these. Watch the people around you. There's so much more than we usually see.

Mental workout 5: Let the story find you

Spend a couple of minutes taking a walk outside (or around the building you're in, if it isn't practicable to go outside). Find an object you can take back to a quiet place. It can be anything – just something portable that catches your eye.

Now take a minute to think of the most bizarre situation you can put this object in. It should be something totally incongruous. Think of the object in a tabloid newspaper headline, something from the sort of publication that's always finding Elvis on the Moon. It could be 'the nutcrackers from outer space' or 'the wallet that ate my hamster' or 'my personal organizer is having a baby'.

Finally, take five minutes to write a short story on this theme. Your story should take the context entirely seriously. It can be in the form of a newspaper article or a narrative. Don't spend ages thinking about it – force yourself to write, whatever drivel you produce.

Despite appearances, this isn't about creative writing – it's the thought process that's important, not what you write. Creativity is all about generating new ideas and concepts that somehow don't quite fit with current thinking. At a later date they will be absorbed into the mainstream, but initially they will often seem odd. The techniques at the start of the chapter are there to help stimulate this sort of idea production. Yet before you can do anything with a technique, you need the ability to detach yourself from a conventional train of thought. Exercises like this are designed to do just that.

There are almost an infinite number of contexts in which you can put any object. These can range from the mundane ('the stone that wasn't there yesterday') to the unusual ('the stone that thought it was the President of the USA'). It's a good idea to keep the context unusual, because that helps force a creative viewpoint.

Mind magic – essentials

Creativity is something you do as a human being, using your brain. It's a natural ability you are born with. Everyone is born with it. But there are plenty of techniques you can use to help make the ideas flow more easily. For instance:

- Blockages
  - Be aware of how you and others block ideas.
  - You *are* creative; don't shoot down your own ideas.
  - Give ideas a chance to grow before you decide whether they are good or bad.
  - You don't need to be an expert. Some of the best ideas come from people who don't know what's not possible.
  - Don't be scared of coming out with an idea just because you might sound stupid.

- Go for a walk. Get away from distractions for a few minutes and let your mind wander. It's a great way to have ideas.
- Use a random picture. Note what the picture makes you think of, then work through each of these thoughts and see how they could help with your problem or need for an idea.
- Use attributes. List the main attributes of the situation you are trying to change. Then try modifying those attributes one at a time and see what the change suggests.
- Use reversal. See how you could achieve the opposite of what you want to do, then make use of those suggestions to think up new ways of getting to your goal.
- Be someone else. Look at the problem through another character's eyes – someone as far away from the problem as you can think of – and use their insights to come up with new ideas.
- Give yourself a boost. Get some fresh air, a sugar shot, or mental stimulation by stumbling on something new on the web, reading a short story or listening to a new piece of music.
- Don't try to take off the wheel nuts with your bare hands. Take the time to take a step back, think about what you are doing and use the right tool for the job.
- Use regular mental exercises to help keep your brain in shape.
- Take a look at other techniques and software to help with creativity.

Chapter 3

An original approach

Ever heard someone say, 'It's what's inside that counts'? They mean you shouldn't judge by appearances. It's the person inside that matters, the personality that's important, not the looks. And that's great when you are dealing with human relationships, but it's not so good when it comes to presenting your ideas. Like it or not, it is going to matter how you present your work. Creativity isn't just for getting the ideas themselves, it comes into every aspect of the way you structure and present information. Let's start prettifying.

Personal without the weird

We all know people who have a very individual approach to life. Fashion isn't their thing; they wear what they want to wear, whatever anyone else thinks. Some people (not always the same people) take the same approach to the way they personalize their work. They don't worry about the conventions, they do it their way. How much you can get away with this depends on who you are and what you are doing. The poet e. e. cummings was able to get away with his trademark avoidance of capital letters – but it's not something most of us would be sensible in doing when handing in a piece of work, unless it is very specifically and clearly illustrating a point. (To be honest, even cummings' use of the technique looks rather pretentious and childish now.)

Similarly, you might love feathers and feel the urge to decorate your physics report or your history dissertation with a nice feathered border. Best not. Even if the person who will be reading your work isn't allergic to birds, it's the sort of personalization that just comes across as odd (unless you are under 13).

Yes, make the work, including the presentation style, your own, but do it in a subtle and sophisticated way. If the effect is to put the reader off, it doesn't matter how good the content is, or how clever the presentation idea seemed to you at the time, it will do you no good. So if you get a weird urge – for instance, 'I'll smear my sociology report with dog faeces to show how corrupt society is!' – make sure you that repress the urge and think about how the lecturer, tutor or teacher is going to react.

Building your structure

Before we get on to the detailed layout, it's worth giving a little thought as to how you are going to structure your content. Construct a quick outline. For each chapter (if there are chapters), or under the main title, put in a series of subtitles for the different sections of the document. This doesn't mean you have to have subtitles in the finished report (though they can be handy); you can always delete them later, but for now they are acting as markers, showing what goes where in your structure.

There's a chance here to be creative. With some tasks, the obvious structure is usually the best one. Biography and history, for instance, often benefit from a chronological structure. But not always. When I wrote my biography of the pioneer of motion pictures Eadweard Muybridge, *The Man Who Stopped Time*, I made the subject of the first chapter an incident that happened when he was in his forties. This is because it was a hugely influential and dramatic moment in his life. It was then that he discovered that he was not the father of his child. As a result, he tracked down and murdered his wife's lover.

At the end of that first chapter, with Muybridge in jail awaiting trial, I could then slip back to his birth, as if he was thinking back over his life so far. Taking this sort of approach has two benefits. First of all, it's a teaser. It gives you a hint of what's to come. And second, it really gets the reader engaged with the story. Starting with historical context and someone's birth is often more than a trifle dull.

One useful way of thinking about how to structure something is to think how a good movie might portray the story. In Muybridge's case I think it would almost certainly start with the murder. I stress the word 'good' there. Some biographical films jump back and forth in time, going all over the place and leaving the viewer totally confused. You don't want what you've written to have the same effect. Using a structure that doesn't work solidly chronologically from beginning to end should be done to encourage the reader in, but not just to show off how clever you are.

While chronological structuring often makes sense, it certainly isn't the only option. You might use some sort of categorization. For example, if you were writing something about musical instruments, you could divide your work up by the different types of instrument (woodwind, brass, percussion, etc.), or by their physical position in the orchestra, just as easily as by the date when the particular instrument was introduced.

If you are writing something with a number of people at its heart, then a person-by-person approach might work better than a chronological one – as long as it doesn't become a dull string of people like a biographical dictionary.

Generally, when you are structuring writing, it's a bit like writing a piece of music. You want to engage the reader, pull them along, get them wanting to get on to the next piece. One way to do this is to break your work into relatively short chunks. If it's a long dissertation, don't have a very few, extremely long chapters, but break it up more. Each chunk or chapter should have its own internal structure: a beginning that leads you in, a central core and an end that is leading the readers on to the next chunk, perhaps giving a glimpse of what's coming, encouraging them to read on.

A specific consideration when structuring is the peripheral bits and pieces. Should you have a contents page? Certainly if the document is large enough to require it – say 10 pages or more, or if you have been asked to include one. For shorter documents they aren't usually necessary. Only go for one if there are a lot of small segments that need an overview, or a way of jumping into them.

How about an introduction? Yes, if it's a good way to draw people in, giving them a taste of what's coming up. But please don't stick in one of the dull introductions you often see in non-fiction books that most readers skip because they provide either a detailed summary of the contents or a way for the author to show off. Conclusions are more important. Even if you don't have a separate concluding chapter (and often these can seem a little thin if they are included), you should have at least a paragraph or two at the end of the main text that pulls it all together. Without that, you haven't got a clear sense that the document is finished. The conclusion both helps the reader revise what they've read, and makes a clear announcement that the end has been reached. Putting in 'The End' looks childish; a clear conclusion makes it obvious you've got to the finish without being so blatant.

After that, you may be required to provide notes, citations and a bibliography. Do what is asked of you, but no more. As for an index, provide one if necessary, but be very clear why it's there. Indexes can be very useful, but only if you are writing the sort of document someone is going to look things up in. A good index takes quite a lot of effort to put together. Only do one if you are required to, or if the book will need this kind of reference.

If you are producing an index, there are two ways it could be used. One is for someone to come and look up something in isolation. Say you've written a long piece about the French Revolution. I might want to check out what happened to the chemist Lavoisier, so I would go to the index and look for 'Lavoisier'. The other use needs a rather different style of entry. I might already have read the document, and want to go back to a particular place. For this type of index searching, it's important to have entries in your index that will stick in the memory. Because of the nature of memory (see Chapter 5), these will tend to be bits of the text involving people, or something dramatic or visual. So be prepared to put items in your index that are fairly peripheral to the story, but that will catch the memory when your reader is trying to revisit a piece of text. Take a look at this text from my previous book, *Studying Using the Web*:

> Look out also for opportunist sites that load a page with lots of words that aren't particularly relevant. The Christina Aguilera result (number 7), for example, is highly unlikely to tell you a lot about Elizabethan composers. With a bit of eye training, you will find it easy to home in on the sites that are most likely to come with a valuable result. At first glance, in the list above, I would take a look at numbers 1, 2, 4, 6 and 8.

This section of the book was on how to filter search results to find the most useful content, and the search in question was on Elizabethan church music, yet one of the things I indexed from this page was Christina Aguilera. That's because if you wanted to get back to this page, you would find it hard to pin down exactly what words to look for (and the church music topic was referred to in several places), but this is the only place in the book where I refer to Christina Aguilera, so it might well stick in the mind ('I want to find that bit that mentioned Christina Aguilera'), so into the index she goes. It helps that she's a name from pop culture; they will often stick in the mind.

Finally, a valuable tool in structuring your work is mind mapping. We will cover mind mapping in detail in the next chapter, so don't worry if it doesn't mean much to you at the moment, but the advantage of mind mapping, particularly when you are using a piece of software, is the ease with which you can move the structure around until it is ideal.

Hold the layout

When it comes to deciding what goes where on the page, you have plenty of opportunity to exercise that creativity that you've been holding back to avoid being too original and putting your reader off. Check that you haven't been given any layout specifications – but if it's down to you, then get ready to sparkle. There are no great rules for many of the layout decisions you will have to make. If you want, for example, a picture to go to the right or the left of the text – or in the middle, for that matter – it's entirely up to you. But there are some handy rules you can use to check out your layout and make sure it will be appreciated. Specifically:

- **Don't overdo the title.** If you use something like WordArt (see page 58) to produce a fancy title, don't let it take over the page. On a normal page the title should stand out clearly, but shouldn't dominate, or you won't get a feel for the content. Try to keep the title to the top inch (2.5 cm) of content. This doesn't apply if you have a separate title page – then you can go as large as you like.
- **Be careful about columns.** It's easy to get carried away with columns, making your pages like over-busy newspapers. Lots of columns are fine if you are printing on paper the size of a newspaper, but for ordinary paper, either avoid columns or consider having one main column with either one or two sidebars. These are relatively narrow columns down one or both sides which will carry asides, notes and shorter pieces of information. Sometimes sidebars are given a light background shading to make them stand out.
- **Don't use text justification.** Most word processors have an option to 'justify' the text so that it aligns up with both margins, as in a book such as this. Usually, though, the way the word processor puts gaps in the sentences to spread them out looks messy. There's no need to use full text justification in an ordinary document.

- **Let text wrap around pictures.** Modern word processors don't merely let you put pictures into a document, but also let you wrap text around them, so that there aren't big empty spaces alongside the illustration. Make use of this facility; it usually improves the look of a page.
- **Don't use too many pictures.** If you are writing the kind of document that needs illustrations, don't go mad with them. Typically, two to three pictures a page is a sensible maximum, otherwise there isn't room for the accompanying text. Don't be tempted to make the pictures too big, either, unless the picture itself is an important part of your material.
- **Look how the professionals do it.** Take a look at a number of text-oriented magazines and business leaflets to get some layout hints.
- **Be consistent.** Once you have decided on a basic layout style for a page, keep it the same all the way through the document. Of course, later pages might bring in new elements (pictures, say) that weren't in that first page, so you may need to modify the style, but don't make dramatic changes.

If in doubt, put your word processor into a view that lets you see the whole of a page at once. Take a look at it as a whole, without reading individual bits of text. How does it look? Is it top-heavy? Does the layout look smart or straggly? Does it seem to be over-heavy on one side or the other? Fine-tune how it looks, based on your overview of the page.

Another consideration on layout is line spacing. If you haven't been asked to provide a document double-spaced (i.e. with a blank line between each line so there's room to write in comments by hand), as you may be required to do for a dissertation, keep it to single spacing. Double-spaced text wastes paper and is harder to read. Between paragraphs, though, it is worth leaving a space (and optionally indenting the first line of the paragraph a little to emphasize that this is a beginning). Don't do this manually; use the paragraph setting on the word processor to change the style of your text so that it automatically includes a line space between paragraphs and an indent at the start. If your word processor has styles, it's worth getting the hang of these and setting up a style for your 'normal' or body text that has this format. That way, if you want to change the layout later, you can just change the style, and the whole document will be altered to match.

One little layout relic from the past is worth putting to rest. You will sometimes find people – often people who were brought up using typewriters, or taught to type by someone who was used to a typewriter – putting two spaces after the full stop (period) at the end of a sentence. This is because of the way a typewriter worked. Typing a full stop and one space didn't leave a big enough gap. Modern word processors use proportional spacing. If you take a look at the letter 'i' in the word 'spacing', it doesn't take up much room at all, while the 'm' in 'room' is much wider. Similarly, a word processor knows to put a bigger space after the end of the sentence. There's no need to double it up (unless you are specifically requested to do so).

Picture this

We've already dipped a toe into the water of using pictures, but now let's get specific. First we've got to get over a touch of snobbery. Because children's books have lots of pictures in and many adult books don't have illustrations, there's a bit of a feeling that there's something inferior about using pictures. Forget it. Pictures work. If you look in a serious academic science journal such as *Nature*, it is just as full of pictures these days (some of them very beautiful) as is a Sunday supplement.

However, this isn't an open invitation to use pictures everywhere and anywhere. The important thing before sticking in a picture is to ask, 'What does it do?' Don't just add a picture for the sake of it; be clear what the picture is there for. It might be to provide an attractive, eye-catching opener. It might be to illustrate a particular point in your text, or to act as a sort of visual punctuation mark. All that is fine. Just make sure you know why it's there. If the picture doesn't add anything to the text, get rid of it.

A final quick tip on pictures: make sure that the picture does the job in the finished format. Take a look at it in print (assuming this is a printed document) before you decide for certain whether or not to use it. I read a book the other day called *The Creation* by E. O. Wilson. A lot of effort has gone into the look and feel of the book, but someone hadn't done the check I'm suggesting, and that resulted in one frustratingly disastrous image. There's a map that's labelled something like 'Thirty-four of the most critical biodiversity hotspots'. I've no doubt the original version showed just that. But in the book, however much you peer at it, you just see a plain, featureless map of the world. Not a hotspot in sight. No doubt they were there on the original big image on someone's computer, but by the time it had been sized down and printed on the page, the hotspots were invisible.

A font of knowledge

Once upon a time, fonts were only a matter of concern for printers (I mean the people who did printing for a living, not the box attached to your computer) and those who invested in sheets of Letraset, or similar rub-on lettering to produce posters and fancy headlines. Everyone else used whatever was on the typewriter – typically something like the Courier font.

When Macs and Windows came along, all that changed. Suddenly there was a wild and wonderful outbreak of fonts. Scanning down the font list on my word processor, I've about 200 available to me. Having all those fonts is very tempting. It seems a great chance to really make your work stand out. But there's a real danger of making it less readable instead.

Three simple rules will help keep those overactive fonts from taking over and ruining your work.

First, use only two fonts per document: one for the main text, the other for titles, headlines, and the like. You can use different variants (see below) for different levels of heading – perhaps a significantly bigger bold version for the main or chapter title and bold italics, slightly bigger than the body text, for the section titles – but don't go mad with different fonts. It's best to keep your body text, the stuff people actually read, in the same font all the way through. The only exception is that you might like to pull out some sections like my 'aside' boxes in a slightly different text – say using sans serif instead of serif, but still using a clear, readable font.

Aside: Serif and sans serif

Sans serif may sound like a small island off the coast of Mexico, but it's just a way of describing the look of some fonts. Mostly, fonts are divided into serif – which have twiddly bits, like the little bar at the bottom of the letter 'I' – and sans serif, which don't have the twiddly bits. The title of this 'aside' box is in a sans serif font (common ones are Arial, Helvetica and Verdana) and the main text of the book is in a serif font (you might be using Garamond, for instance).

Second, make your fonts readable. The essence of readability is not going for fonts that are too fancy. Be very wary of extremely cursive fonts – ones that are all twists and turns, like fancy handwriting – or heavy gothic fonts that look like old German. Generally speaking, if it's not obvious at a glance what a word says, the font is not readable enough.

Third, keep the fancy stuff for posters. This is a different type of font variation. Fonts for posters still need to be very readable, but also to be eye-catching, so there's an excuse for going a little mad with some of the more extravagant fonts out there that look like anything from a woodcut to something assembled from cut-out bits of newspaper. Even here, though, stick to the two-font rule – but you can go a little wilder with those fonts. Occasionally these fancy fonts will be acceptable for the title of a piece of work; it depends on the style of document. If it's a scientific paper, it's best to avoid heading it with Algerian or Jokewood, or one of the other dramatic fonts, but you could use them occasionally in something intentionally bold in appearance.

Just don't go too mad. Use font variation sparingly and you will get a much stronger effect. It's a bit like swearing. If someone swears all the time, it soon doesn't signify anything, but if someone who hardly ever swears does so, it makes you take notice. If you keep your titles sober and stylish, but just occasionally do something dramatic, it will catch the attention much more effectively than if every piece of work has wild and wonderful fonts.

As with all rules, you can break the three rules of font selection where it's appropriate. There will be occasions when you want to slip in an extra font for a special purpose. But if you normally stick to two, you'll know when you need something special and decorative.

Being very bold

Once upon a time, when people had typewriters, not only were they restricted to one font, but also they had very little opportunity to make differences in the way their text looked. The only things you could do on a typewriter were to make the text a bit bolder by going back and typing over it again, or to underline it by going back and typing underline characters (which never made a neat, unbroken line) over the same stretch of text. Incidentally, because of this, underlining became a secret code between writers and printers for italics. If something was underlined, it was meant to be shown in the final version as italics.

With a modern computer you have a vast armoury at your disposal. Taking a quick look at my word processor, I find I can apply at least ten different variants to my basic text, from strikethroughs to an embossed look. Throw in point sizes and being able to use block capitals, and the choice is huge.

As with fonts themselves, the only important rule is not to go over the top with different point sizes and formats. Generally speaking, titles should be larger than the main text. You can make them stand out by using bold. Italics is a bit of a special case. In your body text, this is used either to identify that something is the name of a book or magazine or something similar (as when I refer to my previous book *Studying Using the Web*), or to give a particular word extra or unexpected stress.

In titles, italics can be used for effect. Using italics can be particularly useful if you have three different levels of title. Making the second level italic as well as making it intermediate in size will emphasize which title style you are dealing with.

Give underlining a miss. Underlining isn't normally used in the printed form – take a look at a book or magazine. As we've seen, it was used with a typewriter (or when writing by hand) to stand in for italics. Underlining generally looks messy and should be avoided, even for titles. The only time I'd ever consider making use of underlining is when I am quoting something else – say a handwritten document – and underlining was used in the original.

To an extent, setting something all in capitals is another unnecessary approach. As a typewriter hadn't got different font sizes, it was quite common to put titles all in upper case (perhaps underlined too). These days, using block capitals is often a visual metaphor for shouting in text, which needs to be borne in mind. Terry Pratchett, for example, uses capitals very effectively in his Discworld books for Death's speech, to emphasize its dark, commanding quality. You can use block capitals as one title style – but only if it really looks better than the alternatives. A neat compromise is to set all but the initial letters of a title in small capitals, which can look very striking.

If you really want to go to town on a title, then many word processors have the ability to put in something fancy, for example using WordArt in Word. This lets you use huge letters, distort their shapes, give them fancy colours and so on. As with most presentation style issues, less is more. Only go for multicoloured letters if the use suits the look. Yes, feel free to use WordArt to create an eye-catching main title on the front of your piece, but don't use it for subheadings later on in the piece; that's just too overwhelming for the eye.

Colouring in

With typewriters, colour wasn't much of an issue. Your text was black or black, unless you had a dual-colour ribbon, in which case it was likely to be black or red. Colour can be very effective in text to highlight a point, to really make it stand out, but use it sparingly. It's probably best to stick to a single highlight colour to avoid producing a mess.

The most important consideration, particularly if using coloured backgrounds, is whether or not the colour makes the text illegible. Red text on dark pink backgrounds (yes, I have seen this used) is very difficult to pick out. On the whole it's best to stick to black, dark grey or dark blue text on a light-coloured background, or white text on a dark-coloured background.

There are a few simple rules when dealing with colour.

1 Use colour to increase information content

Colour should always be there for a reason. It's a way of increasing the information content of your page, making it easier for the reader to interpret. Colour coding, for instance, can help the reader realize that different items are part of the same group even when they aren't physically next to each other.

2 Take advantage of the associations of colour

Readers may think of particular meanings when they see a colour, which might be useful to you. Think of red, yellow and green in traffic lights, for instance. Warm hues can produce a positive emotional response while cool hues are more restrained. You need to realize, though, that the associations of colours vary from culture to culture. For example, black is associated with death in the West, but white is the colour of mourning in China. People from equatorial regions prefer brighter, more saturated colours, while muted tones and pastels go down better in temperate latitudes.

3 Allow for the human visual system

Our human eye–brain combination isn't consistent in the way it handles colours. In normal daylight, the eye is most sensitive to yellow and green, and least to red and blue. This means that you should avoid using red and blue for the presentation of fine detail or isolated characters. Combinations of yellow on white and blue on black are particularly bad.

Chromatic aberration in the eye (the way various colours are focused differently by the lens in your eye) causes red and blue to separate in apparent distance. Blue text on a red background is particularly disturbing and should be avoided. The eye can't focus on the edges separating two patches of colour of equal lightness. Try to ensure that adjacent colours have a difference in their lightness. Otherwise, separate the regions with a thin black line. Think cartoon characters, which have a black line surrounding them for this reason.

Large areas of heavy, saturated colour can make the reader's eyes tired. Use more pastel colours for backgrounds and the prominent items. Don't place highly saturated colours side by side.

4 Allow for the limitations of individual readers

We don't all see colours the same way. The way you use colours in your text should take into account how your reader is going to see it.

The age of the reader is important. Children prefer primary colours, adults more muted ones. Older people generally have more trouble in discriminating blue.

About 9 per cent of the male population (and 0.5 per cent of females) have some form of colour blindness. The most common is a confusion of reddish blues with greenish blues and yellowish reds with yellowish greens. Where discrimination is important, opposing red with cyan (turquoise) or yellow with purple will reduce the chances that the colours will be misinterpreted.

Drawing them in

Writing isn't a way of putting letters on a piece of paper for the pure art of it, a sort of two-dimensional sculpture; it's a means of communication. It is intended to get information from one place – your brain – to another – someone else's brain – via the paper or email or whatever it is you are writing.

Because it's communication, you need more than plain information in your writing. What you put down on the page needs to get the information across to the reader. A few simple techniques can help make your writing more readable, and more effective.

1 Keep your sentence short – but not too short

Of course it's perfectly possible to have long, really long, almost impossibly long, sentences that go on and on seemingly for ever until the reader begins to lose the will to live, as this sentence is itself beginning to do . . . but it isn't necessary. Any sentence can be broken up. Of course that doesn't mean you should write like a machine gun. Little short sentences. These break the flow. Irritating. Just keep the sentences to a manageable length for the reader.

2 Be careful with 'he', 'she', 'it' and the like

It can be easy, if you aren't careful, to lose track of what's going on in a piece of text. Take this little example:

> There was little to choose between the different candidates in the election. The polling station was almost empty all day. It was a failure. Smith beat Jones, but only after Edwards was removed from the race. He triumphed, it's true, but his triumph was short-lived. When Jones met him the next day, he was disappointed to see a big smile on his face.

The general rule is that a pronoun like 'she' or 'it' refers to the most recently mentioned person or object. So strictly 'It was a failure' should refer to the polling station (or possibly the day), not the election. Things get horribly confused between Smith, Jones and Edwards in the later part of the paragraph. Who triumphed? Who did Jones meet next day, and who was disappointed to see a big smile on whose face? This paragraph needs recasting to make it clearer who is being referred to:

There was little to choose between the different candidates in this failure of an election. The polling station was almost empty all day. Smith beat Jones, but only after Edwards was removed from the race. Smith triumphed, it's true, but his triumph was short-lived. When Jones met him the next day, Smith was disappointed to see a big smile on his opponent's face.

There is still the odd example of a pronoun there, but it's obvious who the 'his' and the 'him' refers to.

3 Watch out for habitual phrases

We all tend to use certain little words and phrases in the way we speak. Some of us come out with 'you know' or 'um' or 'OK' very frequently without even realizing we're doing it. When I was at university, we had a lecturer who said 'of course' so often that the students starting counting out loud each time he used it. It took a while for him to spot what was happening; when he did, he stopped himself.

On paper, these habitual little phrases tend to be more subtle, but they can still crop up. I have a tendency to use 'in fact' too much. One of the things I do when I'm checking through my work is to look out for this sort of repetition.

4 Read it like a stranger

In fact, checking through your work, which is an essential part of making it readable, is more than just a matter of looking for mistakes. (Did you notice my habitual 'in fact' there?) If you get a chance, leave your work for a day or two (if you don't have that much time, leave it as long as you can), then read it through as if it were written by a stranger. Look out for what reads well and what is clumsy. It can help to read it aloud to get a sense of how it flows.

5 Use variety, but be friendly

Using the same word over and over again is boring. If you wrote something saying 'this is nice, and that's nice; oh, and the other thing is nice too', the reader would quickly get bored with 'nice'. Vary your words. In particular, try not to repeat the same word too near to its first use in a sentence or adjacent sentences. But this doesn't mean using such fancy words that you will irritate your reader. Consider the title of a paper by Princeton psychologist Daniel Oppenheimer that won an Ig Nobel Prize in 2006: 'Consequences of erudite vernacular utilized irrespective of necessity: problems with using long words needlessly'.

6 Lead the reader on

Think how a well-written thriller works. We are shown something exciting and intriguing. We want to read more, to find out why what we saw happened. Our interest and curiosity are engaged. And as we read more, we meet up with further mysteries and little snippets to encourage us further on. It's a page-turner. No one is expecting your dissertation or essay to be a *Da Vinci Code*, but it is possible to learn from this type of book. (This says nothing about whether or not a book like *The Da Vinci Code* is good fiction, or whether you like it. You can still learn from the techniques used by the likes of Dan Brown.) At the end of each section, consider throwing in a little 'teaser' that gives a hint of what's coming up. Give the reader an incentive to carry on reading: make it exciting.

7 Leave them wanting more

'Leave them wanting more' is an old saying from the stage. If you can leave your audience wanting more, you've succeeded. Give them too much, even of great content, and they will lose interest. It's a constant complaint I have when I review books for the Popular Science website. All too often these books are too long, not because the writer has lots of different good things to say, but because he or she has one thing to say, and says it different ways so as to make the book long enough. The same goes for your paper or essay. You need to make it of the required length, but not by repetition. Make sure all the content is essential. Pare it down ruthlessly.

I've hardly ever written something that can't then be cut down to make it read better. Take a look at a simple example I gave in *Studying Using the Web*. It's so easy to have redundant words in your writing.

> **Little, sniveling words that do not really deliver anything more for the text that you have written.** Destroy them mercilessly. Take that previous sentence beginning 'Little, sniveling'. Let's give it a trim. Although it probably wasn't necessary to use both 'little' and 'sniveling' at the start, the two adjectives give the

sentence a kick start and I would like to keep them in. But 'do not' is a little clumsy, and unless I was writing very formally, I think I would prefer 'don't' in this context. That word 'really' does nothing at all for the sentence. It's redundant.

Then what about that 'you have written' bit at the end? Isn't it obvious we're talking about the text you had written? I can gather that from the context. In fact it might be better still to drop 'for the text' as well. Once I've done that, it might be better to change 'more' to 'new'. So I end up with this. **Little, sniveling words that don't deliver anything new**. I have lost 9 words of 17 and produced a sentence that is more pithy, more to the point and more readable.

Be prepared to take out whole sentences too, if they don't add anything. I almost always find that in the first draft of a book I will include something about a topic I'm really interested in, but that doesn't have much to do with the content of the book I'm writing. Sometimes it's just a little fun, like a game I've played with the last few books I've written (even one about the rather heavy-sounding science of quantum entanglement), which was an attempt to mention *Buffy the Vampire Slayer* in each book. But often it's a chunk of text that's only there because I'm interested in the subject. The reader won't be. Cut it out.

8 Pad cautiously

If you have been given a particular length to write to, you may find that you have written something shorter. Don't be tempted to pad it out by reversing the process described above and putting lots of redundant words in. That's feeble. Make sure there's more content going in too. One good way to do this can be to put in supporting matter like my 'Aside' boxes, or tables and other side content. Alternatively, you could develop another significant point. But don't be tempted to add sheer padding.

On paper; on screen

Most of the advice I've given is oriented to the written word on paper, or in a screen equivalent of paper, like an email. But you may also need to create special on-screen text like a PowerPoint presentation. Here there are a number of special rules that apply.

Take particular care with the colour suggestions I made earlier. Colour problems like the difficulty of using blue text on a red background become even worse when they appear on a screen. Making your text legible is more important than making it pretty.

I've seen many, many PowerPoint presentations, and the most common error is trying to get too much information on to a single slide. Text should be in bullet points, using keywords, not great long sentences. The text should be clearly legible anywhere in the room; as a rule of thumb, I wouldn't normally put more than eight lines of text on to a slide. Remember what the words on the slide are for. They are to reinforce what you are saying, to get it to stick in people's minds, not to be read at great length (unless you are providing a quotation you specifically want people to read).

Do make use of diagrams, pictures, etc., but make sure they are easy to see. I have attended lectures where a hugely complex diagram goes up on screen accompanied by a talk something like:

> 'This is the type of circuit used. You can't actually see, but that's the main bus there.' [Points at screen] 'Those four terminals are labelled "red", "green", "blue" and . . .' [Peers at screen] 'I can't quite make it out, I think it's "purple". If the picture was bigger, you could see that this part doubles back on itself, and you might just be able to make out . . .'

And so it goes on. Don't take a diagram from somewhere else and use it on screen unless it's clearly readable.

One slightly surprising little fact: research has shown that serif fonts like Times Roman are more legible on paper, but sans serif fonts like Arial are easier to read from a screen. So make the body text of your on-paper work a serif font, but use a sans serif font for your main text in a presentation.

It also looks good if all the slides in a presentation have a consistent look and feel – the same style of heading, the same background colour, and so on. Don't keep chopping and changing.

All I should be concerned with is the look of your slides – this isn't a book on public speaking – but I can't help throwing in two of the key mistakes made in giving presentations. First, don't read from the slides; your audience can read (or why show them the slide in the first place?). What you say should expand on the bullet points, not repeat them. Second, don't look at the projected slide as you talk. Your audience wants to see your face, not your back. This is a particularly tempting mistake when using a smartboard, as you tend to turn to the board to interact with it. Do whatever you need to do as quickly as possible, then turn back to face the audience. If you can, have a secondary screen you can see when facing the audience, so you don't have to keep looking at the projection.

An original approach – essentials

Presentation might be all about what's on the surface, but good presentation is essential if you want to get your information across. Creativity is just as important here as in the content. Look out for these key points:

- You should aim for a look that's personal but not off-putting.
- See if there's a chance to be creative with the structure – but don't lose the reader in the process.
- Use mind maps or another approach to clarify your structure.
- Make sure your layout makes the content more visible, rather than hiding it.
- Make use of pictures for a purpose, not just for the sake of illustrating.
- Start with a maximum of two fonts per document. Make those fonts readable ones.
- Make use of italics for sources and emphasis, and of bold for titles. Don't use underlining, except when quoting a source that used it.
- Be aware of the effect your choices of colour will have on the reader.
- Make your text more readable by:
  - keeping sentences to a manageable length;
  - making sure it's obvious who a 'he' or 'her' belongs to;
  - cutting out any habitual phrases;
  - reading what you've written as if through the eyes of a stranger;
  - using reader-friendly variety;
  - leading the reader on;
  - leaving them wanting more;
  - being cautious about padding.

- Remember that a document and a PowerPoint presentation need different approaches.

Chapter 4

Mapping the facts

If you're a student, it can seem as though you spend half your life taking notes. Looked at honestly, the way we take notes is pretty antiquated; the only advance from chiselling into tablets of stone or using a slate is that you've got a gel pen and a stylish notebook (or possibly a boring-looking one if you want to make a fashion statement).

Of course, every class or lecture has one person who uses six different-coloured pens and underlines things with rulers – but that's probably not you. What we need to do is go back to the beginning and see what note taking is for, whether we're talking about notes taken in classes or lectures, notes that condense the essential facts from a book, or just notes of your own thoughts and ideas.

Why take notes?

If we had perfect memories, capturing every bit of information we experienced, storing away every thought we had in the right place to recall it whenever it was needed, then we could forget note taking. Notes are there to help your memory, in capturing information both from an outside source (a class or talk or lecture or book) and from inside your brain (your ideas, your reaction to what you hear or read, new thoughts that come out of the information you are getting).

That's the first level of answer to 'Why take notes?' But there's another one too. What do you need to note this information for? If it's an examination, then you will need the notes in a structure that makes it easy to revise – to go back over the information, perhaps many times, until it is forced into your memory, ready for immediate use when required. The same applies if it is information you are going to use in your everyday life; this could be anything from training in cardiopulmonary resuscitation to the essential facts for a car driver. You need to be able to go over that information easily, as many times as it takes to squeeze it into memory.

Alternatively, it could be information you need for a one-off project – something you are going to use once, then quite probably throw in the waste-paper basket. In this case, it's best if you can give the information some kind of top-level structure that fits with your project. You might have lots of detailed notes, but the essential is to be able to pull in the right parts in the right order when you are putting everything together.

Finally, there's squirrelled information. This is stuff that you store away because it might come in useful some day. You don't know when, or exactly for what – but it might prove valuable. There was a time when being an information squirrel was an insult. It implied that someone stored away lots of information but never really did anything with it. That's because in the old days it soon became hard to find anything you had squirrelled away. Now, with properly used computers, it's much easier.

In fact, computers have done away with a big slice of the need to be an information squirrel at all. At one time, for instance, if you were interested in a subject and you got a regular magazine on it, as a good information squirrel you would have had to keep all those magazines stored away in a cupboard somewhere – just in case they came in useful. Now, chances are that that magazine has a web-based archive, and you can look up what you need in back numbers without a single copy being kept. (Sometimes the archives need a subscription to get access, but if you don't subscribe yourself, you can usually get to the archive through a library.)

However, there still are things that fall into that 'might come in useful' category, the mental equivalent of all that lumber in the garage or the attic or the cellar. The important thing here, because it could be months or years before you come back and want to find that information, is to have an easy way of getting to it.

We'll come back to the different ways to structure and search for information in your notes, but first let's revisit the brain, and what we are expecting of it as a result of our note taking.

Kicking the brain into action

As we'll find out in more detail in the next chapter, the brain is not a single lump of stuff all doing the same thing, like a kidney or a liver.

Instead, it is divided into many different functional parts. We saw earlier on how the two halves of the brain seem to have different roles – but both are involved in memory, so one useful approach in trying to get your notes to sink in is to make use of both sides of the brain.

How are you going to do this? The usual business of writing nice straight lines of words comes down heavily on the left-hand side. The right side, which is more responsible for images and touchy-feely stuff, colour and the overview, is likely to give up. To kick it into action it's a good idea to give your notes some features that will need right-brain activity.

That means colour (so those coloured pens weren't so silly). It means visual stuff – little drawings, giving your notes a visual structure on the page with boxes and lines and laying things out differently. And it means overview – having bits of your notes that pull everything together, a bit like the summaries at the end of each chapter in this book. You probably can't do this at the time you make the notes, but it's worth doing the first time you read through them – write yourself a quick overview.

If we can pull in the right-hand side of the brain, the memories are more likely to stick and be easy to recall. There are different parts of the brain that handle different types of memory. Your short-term, working memory sits at the front of the brain, while your long-term memory is tucked away deep inside. To get information from one to the other takes some action. Again we'll look at ways to actively make your memory better in the next chapter, but for the moment, when we look at your notes, we want to make sure they are well suited to stimulating the memory.

Layout, highlight, illustrate

To get information into such a form that the brain is more likely to take it in, there are three simple steps.

First, consider the layout. Structure information on your page to help your brain process the information. One way is a mind map (see below). Alternatively, you might just use a simple outline format – a series of key headings on the page, under which you write your notes. Or perhaps a set of boxes. Try different methods to find which suits you best. But make sure there is some sort of layout to your notes. Leave a reasonable amount of white space on the page; this is what helps guide your eye around the structure. If you cram the page full of text, nothing will stand out.

Of course you can help things along a bit, as far as making things stand out go. With just your normal note-taking pen or pencil you can use boxes and underlining to pick out headings or emphasize important text. Develop some special marks of your own to make it easy to zoom in on the essentials. If I've taken a page full of notes and there are a couple of points I want to stand out for immediate action, I put a pair of asterisks surrounded by a squashed circle next to them. My eye is immediately drawn to this symbol when I come back to the notes.

Even better, go one stage further and use a highlighter – but don't go mad. I've seen notes that are totally covered in different colours of highlighters. Once this happens, the highlighters aren't doing their job. The whole point of highlighted text is that it should stand out from the rest. It should be identifying the key words, or a sentence here and there that you want to jump out. Use different colours if you can. You could use one colour for titles, another for key phrases and a third for urgent action, for instance.

Highlighters are good because they add colour to your notes, and this gets the right side of the brain waking up. Even better for this is the use of pictures. You don't have to be a great artist; just a quick picture to illustrate a point can be really effective to make your notes more meaningful. This is another reason for leaving plenty of white space: if your text is too crammed together, you won't have room to illustrate.

Going to the next level: mind maps

If you want to take more effective notes, and to get more benefit out of them afterwards, there is a different method of note taking that many people find useful that is formally called cognitive mapping. The best-known type of cognitive mapping is the mind map, which was devised by Tony Buzan. These visual methods for structuring information are also sometimes called spider diagrams. (If you want to find out more about mind maps, take a look at one of Buzan's books – try *The Mind Map Book* (BBC Books, 2003) or *How to Mind Map* (HarperCollins, 2002).)

There are several benefits to using a mind map to structure your information. First, because it combines shapes and text, a mind map gets all of your brain functioning. Doing so helps produce more creative results, and will also make it easier for you to cram the information into your memory, so that your notes become a much more practical tool for remembering information.

Second, it's much easier to slot new items into a mind map as you think of them than it is with conventional linear notes, or a standard outline structure. The map grows organically.

Finally, you can condense a huge amount of information into a very limited space. Let's imagine I am drawing a map of the idea of mind maps themselves. I start by taking a sheet of paper and turning it through 90 degrees, so instead of the normal 'portrait' way we use paper to write on, I'm using it 'landscape'.

In the middle of the sheet of paper I draw a blob (an oval, say), in which I write the title. From that central blob I draw out thick branches, heading in different directions, but ending up as horizontal lines I can write above (that's why the paper is landscape: to fit in all those horizontal branches). Above each branch I write my outline heading.

If I want to have sub-headings, I draw smaller twigs, growing from the branches, and write a sub-heading over each one. As I think of new headings, I can just slot them in the right place. If I end up with all the branches clustered in one corner, I can redraw the map (this is one of the advantages of using software to draw your mind maps, as the software will automatically balance up your map for you). At this stage, my map looks something like this (I've used a piece of software to make it look neater, but it could just as easily have been hand-drawn):

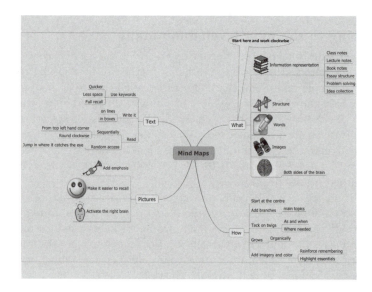

To read the map, after looking at the title in the centre, you read clockwise around the map from the top right-hand corner – so I start from the heading 'What', carry on to 'How', and so on. I've put in the fancy little speech bubble to show where to start because I'm illustrating how mind maps work. You wouldn't normally do this when taking notes, but do keep the same flexibility when it comes to making a few highlighting additions to the map structure. If there's something you want to make stand out, or something that's just a stand-alone fact, pop it in as a floating box.

In the example above, I've intentionally used little graphics in two of the sections, and not in the other two. Even though these seem trivial, I think the example clearly demonstrates how the graphics work (partly just in providing clear space and labelling), as the sections with graphics stand out better than the other two.

Hitting the category

To use mind maps – or any other form of structured note taking – well, it's useful to get a grip on the way we categorize things.

Although the brain probably doesn't use categories to store information in quite the same way as we do consciously, using categories is still an essential if you are going to break down concepts and facts to make them easier to understand. Sometimes categories are obvious. They may be 'good' or 'bad', or simple context categories like 'brand of cosmetic' or 'type of website'. In other cases, the right categories to use don't spring to mind. Here's a little technique that will help in such circumstances.

Spend a minute or two jotting down bullet points from the information. See if you can find key aspects of the information – specific facts or snippets – that can stand alone. Now take three of these items at random. You could use a spreadsheet or write your items on cards to do this. See if you can find a feature that two items share, but the third doesn't. Note down this feature as a category.

Select three at random again and repeat the process several times. There is no right or wrong number of times; do it until you seem to be running out of new categories or you've got at least ten categories.

Look through the categories list, seeing if any of them sensibly combine. Then try to put all the items of information into the different categories. You may need to revisit category generation if you don't have a good set, but it's surprising how often you will have.

Doing this won't generate every possible category – but you are simply trying to find a structure that works. Just as most problems have many solutions, most information can be structured in many different ways. If you are comfortable with the outcome, the categories are fine. With a little practice the categories often come together without your needing this technique, but it's a good way to get started if you have trouble generating categories. It can be used for everything from structuring information to generating an outline for a report.

If you don't have a set of information you need to structure right now, spend a minute writing down at least ten reasons why you like your favourite thing, and use those instead to get the practice.

Is writing necessary?

Even with fancy add-ons like mind maps, writing is pretty old-fashioned. We have the technology these days to take direct 'notes' using a voice recorder or a video camera. So can we throw away that notebook? Probably not.

First, there are many circumstances in which you just can't use these electronic aids. Second, it's a time-consuming way to make notes, because you are going to have to play through the whole thing again to get back to the information you want – and you will probably end up copying out the important stuff on to paper or into a computer at that point. And third, in limiting yourself to capturing a sound-track, you are failing to use the most powerful bit of technology you own: your brain. Normally, when you take notes, you don't just copy word for word, but condense down, refine, connect. None of this happens in a recording. It's just the plain, vanilla original.

This isn't to say that recording is always a disaster for note taking. Many MP3 players and personal digital assistants (PDAs) have the ability to take short voice notes at the click of a button. This is useless for recording a lecture (apart from anything else, the microphone is usually nowhere near good enough), but it's great if you just want to capture a thought when you are walking somewhere or on a bus or generally unable to write something down.

There's also the special case of a lecture or talk that's a one-off special you want to get a lot out of. Then, if possible, it's worth recording the event. If you do this, you can spend most of your time in the actual lecture just listening, taking it in, really absorbing it. Just make a few key notes of essentials you want to come back to.

Then after the event you can go through the recording or video and make detailed notes. If there is a guest speaker, it's not unusual for the school or university to record the lecture for posterity. If you know that's happening, you could get hold of a copy and not have to worry about recording it yourself.

Doing it on the computer

Paper is still hugely useful. When computers really started taking off, people talked about 'paperless offices' and 'paperless schools' where everything would be done electronically. Actually, the reverse has happened. We're using more paper than ever, because it's so easy to print things. And even though a lot of your work will now be done on a computer, you still can't beat a piece of paper or a notebook for a very quick note, or for playing around with ideas in a totally unconstrained way.

It would be silly, though, to write about note taking without looking at what computers can do to help. You can take your notes directly into a computer. Unless you are working at a desk, this means at the very least having a laptop, and even those can be difficult to use in a lot of places you might want to take notes. The smallest, most portable option is a PDA. PDAs started off as electronic address books and diaries, but now offer a whole host of other features.

PDAs aren't bad for scribbling down the sort of quick note you would otherwise use a scrap of paper for, but they aren't ideal for taking pages of lecture notes. The screen is too small to cope with the range of note taking you are likely to want to do. But there is an alternative: tablet PCs.

In principle, these should be the ideal answer, and if they were cheap enough, I'd really recommend that everyone who needs to take notes should have one. They are full-power PCs built into a screen around the size of a sheet of Legal or A4 paper (though a lot thicker). Instead of using a keyboard, you make notes on the screen with a stylus. There's no doubt that tablet PCs are a great idea. Unfortunately, they are typically priced about ten times too much for them to be to be popular. If the price could ever be made manageable, they would be great note-taking tools.

Using software doesn't stop with basic note taking, though. If you like mind maps, you will love mind-map software. There's no doubt that a map from software looks much more effective than a handwritten one, and there's the huge benefit of being able to rearrange the items on the map as and when you want to by dragging them into place with the mouse. The software isn't so good for initial note taking in a lecture – you might still want to draw a map by hand for that – but it's fine for note taking from books, and excellent once you've got some information you want to structure and remember.

Aside: OneNote

Microsoft was the main driving force behind tablet PCs, and early on produced a piece of software called OneNote that really is excellent for note taking. Although designed for use on tablets, it works equally well on an ordinary PC. It is like an enormous electronic notebook. You can type (or write with a stylus on a touch screen) anywhere on the page, and lay things out just as you would in a paper notebook, but then the electronic extras start to come in.

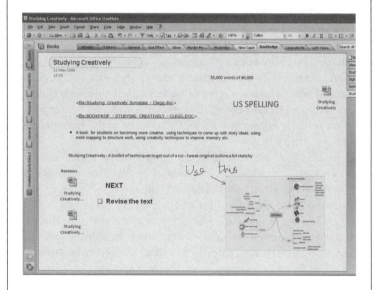

The screenshot above shows a OneNote page used during development of this book.

If you use OneNote to record a talk while you make written notes, then as you play back the recording, your notes are highlighted at the same time in the talk as you made them – sort of karaoke note taking. You can search anywhere in the notes, and put links in so you can jump from one item to another. You can put pictures, or whole documents, into pages. And you can clip items from the web, automatically capturing the web address you copied the information from. If you use your PC a lot for note taking, it's surprisingly good.

For our purposes, mapping software is particularly useful because you can go deeper than just the basic map. Any item in the map can have notes attached, or can have links to web pages. The computer-based map can be used either to give a hand-drawn mind map a better look and structure, or to take notes from something that doesn't need a hand-drawn original, like a book. The simple action of re-structuring your notes into a mind map this way will help fix the information in your brain.

There are several software programs available for structuring information using mind maps or other types of cognitive map. You will find up-to-date information comparing the latest products at www.cul.co.uk/software (click on 'Idea structuring software'). For now, though, let's take a quick look at two products.

The first is Freemind. This is the simplest of the idea mapping packages but has two big advantages. First (as the name suggests), it's free. Second, it's available for pretty well every computer, whether you are running Windows, Mac OS or Linux. Since it is free, there really is no excuse for not giving Freemind a quick try. You'll find it, and more information on how to use it, at freemind.sourceforge.net.

Here's how that same map we used above would look if we're working on it in Freemind (see the illustration on the following page).

Like any piece of software, it takes a bit of getting used to, but once you are used to it, it's very quick to add in text and make a map of your ideas.

Perhaps the biggest problem with Freemind is that it doesn't have a facility to automatically balance a map so that all the branches aren't bunched up on one side; you have to rearrange it yourself.

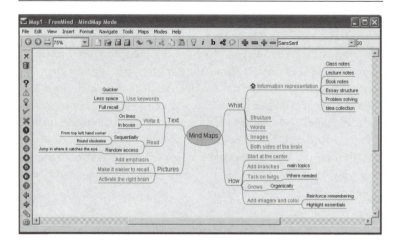

If you find you really like using idea-mapping software and want to go further, the other product that's worth a mention here is MindManager. This is software that you have to pay for, but it's the mind-mapping equivalent of Word or Excel: it's very much the leader of the pack. MindManager was used to produce the maps used to illustrate mind maps on page 70. You can find out more about MindManager at the website www.mindjet.com – and take a free trial of the software.

Mapping the facts – essentials

Taking notes is something we all have to do, whether it's in classes or lectures, or in our everyday life. Although it might seem that note taking is such a basic activity that no one needs any help with it, in fact it's something that can be hugely improved with just a little effort.

- Why take notes?
  - As a prompt to memory.
  - To revise for an examination.
  - To gather information for a project or dissertation.
  - To squirrel away information that might come in useful.

- Using both sides of the brain in notes – making them visual, colourful, pictorial – helps the brain retain the information.
- Layout: structure your page, and don't cram in too much.

- Highlight: pick out key words or essential phrases. Don't highlight too much.
- Illustrate. However weak your drawing skills, pictures make the notes better. Leave plenty of space for them.
- Try out mind maps – for many, they are the ultimate note-taking tool.
- Computers are often best for structuring and reformatting notes, but aren't always ideal for taking the notes in the first place.

Chapter 5

Memories are made of this

Everyone says, 'Studying shouldn't be all about remembering facts.' That's true. But it doesn't stop it being important to be able to memorize a script or a set of historical dates or a vocabulary or a scientific formula if you want to get through your exams. And it can be really helpful in life to remember things. Not just shopping lists, but people or ideas . . . However you look at it, memory is more than a little useful.

The mind maps we tried out in the previous chapter are one good way to help your memory do its job. By laying out the information you want to remember in a mind map, you can give your brain a better chance of taking it in. But there are plenty more techniques to help with memory, some of which have been around for so long that the ancient Greeks used them.

It's really strange, considering how important memory is, and how long memory techniques have been around, that there aren't school lessons on how to help our memories work better. I think maybe it's because these techniques were associated with music hall and vaudeville acts many years ago – 'The Great Memory Man' or whatever. Check out one of the movie versions of *The 39 Steps* if you want to get the idea. Because of these acts, which always depended on memory techniques, doing anything to enhance memory was treated as something normal people didn't do. And that's a shame, because it's very easy to learn techniques that will give you the ability to remember a long string of numbers or a list of facts almost as quickly as you can read them.

Brains aren't computers

You've already found out some useful facts about the brain that help show how to come up with good ideas. Now you've got to dip inside your skull again (just metaphorically: no surgery involved) to look at how your memory works. Thinking sensibly about the brain is harder than it used to be, thanks to computers. We might not be computer experts, but everyone knows about computer memory, all those little bits of information stored on chips in nice, ordered ranks – and it's tempting to think of the brain's memory as being something similar. But it isn't. It's much messier.

First of all, there's more than one kind of memory. In fact, there are three, each primarily the responsibility of a different bit of the brain (though, as we've seen, no activity can be pinned down solely to a particular brain region – other brain parts are involved as well).

Short-term memory sits up behind your forehead in a bit of the brain called the pre-frontal cortex. This is your working memory, those handful (around seven) of slots in which you can temporarily store something until you are ready to either use it or commit it to longer-term memory. Things slip in and out of short-term memory with great ease.

It's a bit harder to get information into *long-term memory*. This is located deeper in the brain in a part that's called the hippocampus. (It looks a tiny bit like a seahorse, if you've a lot of imagination. The word 'hippocampus' is from the Greek name for a seahorse.) Before something can be wedged into long-term memory we need to process it in ways we'll come back to in a moment.

Finally, there's a third type of memory that's altogether more low level. It's sometimes called the *procedural memory*, whereas the other two are called *declarative* (but don't worry too much about that). This memory lies at the 'root' of the brain, in the cerebellum and the top of the spinal cord. This is memory not for facts, but for 'how to do things', and is much quicker to use than the ordinary memory. When you learn to do something well so that you don't really have to think about how to do it – walking, driving a car, typing on a key-board, using a cellphone – it is shifted into this more reflexive memory, meaning that you just get on and do it. A new driver has to think about everything, consulting his or her normal long-term memory, and so is slow to respond, especially when under pressure. It's only when the procedural memory is in charge that we can do things easily and fluidly.

The procedural memory isn't really our concern here. Memorizing facts is the process of shifting things from short-term to long-term memory. And again we have to remember that the brain isn't a computer. A fact isn't remembered as a series of bits, like a word is in a computer memory chip. Our memories are more like an interweaving set of chains. We don't have a database-style index to our memories; we access them through links. One memory sparks another. Images help us locate facts. Everything is much more interconnected and complex. The reason memory techniques work is that they help us to build the links, set up the chains that will hold a piece of information in place and help us to retrieve it.

Pick a number, any number

The simplest information you are liable to need to remember is a number. After all, there are only 10 digits to choose from – how difficult can it be? Actually, that's the problem. Individual numbers don't have a lot of meaning to us, and they're all pretty much the same. To get to know a number, you have to get a little intimate with it. You need to become more than a passing acquaintance, as you probably are with your home phone number, but many of us aren't with our mobile phone number. Let's take an example, the number 34196301793. Take a quick look at it, then read on.

That number is too long to fit one digit in each space in your short-term memory. By the time you have got to the last digit you will have forgotten what the first one was. Yet I can remember what that number is without looking back at it, and using only my short-term memory. How? By using the trick that telephone companies have used for years to make telephone numbers more memorable: breaking them down into pieces. Look at a London telephone number: 020–7870–9557 and a New York number: (646) 257–4068. In each case, the standard way of breaking them up helps the memory. I don't need to remember the first digits of the New York number individually if I know it's that particular NY code.

In fact, when the UK's phone numbers were changed, the (fictional) number shown went from 0171–870–9557 to 020–7870–9557, and in doing that the people issuing the numbers forgot what grouping was about. It was easy to remember 0171 as central London – now we've got the 020 group for London, but the 7 has strayed into the next group and gets lost. It's harder to remember the new numbers. Even worse are mobile (cellphone) numbers, which have no standard way of breaking them up, so hardly anyone can ever remember them.

Let's go back to that number I first came up with. It was 341963 01793. I remembered that because I only actually had to remember three things: the number of a house I used to live in – 34; the year President Kennedy was shot (or *Dr Who* was first broadcast, for TV science fiction nerds) – 1963; and the phone dialling code for the UK town of Swindon, which I happen to know is 01793. Of course, I cheated. I made up a number from shorter numbers that I already had a way of remembering. But it is often possible to break down a number into chunks that do mean something to us – and then it's much easier for us to hold them in our short-term memory to briefly make use of them.

More often, though, we want to cram a number into long-term memory to be able to get it back whenever we like. Long-term memory isn't 100 per cent reliable. A number of years ago I was in a hotel room and my mind went totally blank over my own home phone number. I only managed to remember it when I stopped trying and did something else. Famously, Albert Einstein was always forgetting personal details. He once rang his office to ask where he lived, as he had forgotten the address. (Unfortunately, they told him they weren't allowed to give out Professor Einstein's home address.) But even though long-term memory has these glitches, on the whole it's pretty good, and well worth the effort of getting a number fixed in place. We'll look at a few different ways to do this, starting with perhaps the strangest.

What is this garbage?

Here's a useful little piece of poetry I've just written that's worth committing to memory:

> Wow, I have a rhyme installed in memory,
> Woven, one piece, stunning, brilliant . . .

OK, it's not great verse. In fact, I admit, it's terrible. I never even got as far as rhyming (which is just as well, as there's not that much you can rhyme with memory). But though it is bad literature, it's quite a useful little verse. Counting the letters in each word gives you 3141592653589, which with a helpfully placed decimal point becomes 3.1415926535789 – about as many decimal places of the number π (pi) as any normal person might need to remember. There are plenty of other rhymes for remembering π out there (and, I admit, most are better); I just wanted to show that I could put one together myself without too much effort.

So next time you need to remember a number, instead of committing the whole thing laboriously to memory, you could instead write yourself a little rhyme or phrase with the right number of letters in each word to correspond to the digits in your number. It might seem as though this is a bit like building an electric drill by hand from individual components just to put a small hole in a piece of wood, but there is a point. Although there seems to be much more to remember in a rhyme or phrase, our memories are significantly better at remembering anything that bears a resemblance to a story than they are to remembering something as unnatural as numbers.

Human beings *are* storytellers. It's one of the handful of defining characteristics that makes us human. Until printed books came along, the only means of mass communication was storytelling. We think in terms of stories. A story can make you laugh, or cry. So, a little story is much easier to fix in memory than a set of funny squiggles like numbers that don't really do a lot for us.

This technique works perfectly well, but there are two problems with it. First, it's slow and quite difficult to do. As my example shows – and that took quite a lot of effort, believe it or not – it's not always easy to string together a series of meaningful words of the right length. And then there's the problem of our memory's fuzziness. Mostly when I learn a piece of text, it's not the end of the world if I accidentally say 'Wow, I have a poem installed in my memory' instead of 'Wow, I have a rhyme installed in memory', but in this case I've suddenly changed the first eight digits of π from 3.1415926 to 3.1414922 – which just isn't right. Luckily, there is another way to force numbers into memory that takes less effort and is more reliable.

Here's one I remembered earlier

There's only one problem with this technique: you have to learn ten key words up front before you do anything else. This just takes good old repetition. Keep coming back to them. Recite them in your head. Keep at it until your response is automatic; it won't take long, and you'll be able to use it the rest of your life. Here are the words. Each is associated with one digit:

One – GUN

Two – SHOE

Three – TREE

Four – DOOR

Five – HIVE

Six – STICKS

Seven – HEAVEN

Eight – WEIGHT

Nine – LINE

Ten (0) – HEN

So, your first task is just to get each of these words associated in your mind with the number. Start now. One great way to do this is to draw yourself a set of pictures. Draw the object, and put the number alongside, or intertwined with the object. It doesn't matter how bad your drawings are, as long as you know what they are supposed to be. Recite them too. You'll have noticed the cunning way each number rhymes with the word. Going through the rhymes aloud makes it easier to remember them.

Once you have really got those rhyming words fixed in your mind against the numbers (it might take a day or two; just keep at it), you can use them to remember numbers like phone numbers or PIN numbers or locker numbers or π – or any of the other numbers we all have to remember in seconds. Here's how you do it: you make up a story. Remember, stories are very powerful. As you might guess, you make up a story using the magic words we've listed above. They appear in the story in the order they are in the number. But there is more to it than that.

When you make up that story, you are going to use another feature of the way your brain stores things away. Not only does it make use of stories and chains of information, but also it uses things like visual imagery and colour to fix things in memory. Broadly speaking, the more dramatic, colourful, visual and striking you can make the story you put together in your mind, the easier it will be to fix it in memory. Use gross imagery. Use rude imagery. Use over-the-top, exaggerated pictures in your mind. That's how you can make it stick.

One last thing: usually, you aren't remembering a number in isolation. Start the story with the person or thing your number is associated with. If it's a person's phone number, then start with that person, preferably dressed in a very memorable way, or doing something very strange. If, say, you are trying to remember Planck's constant for a physics exam, think of a plank of wood – but make it a huge, purple plank of wood.

Let's see that in action. Imagine I wanted to remember 4372, which, let us suppose, is the PIN number for my bank card.

So, to remember 4372, the magic words that instantly spring to my mind, because I've got these rhymes really well embedded, are DOOR, TREE, HEAVEN, SHOE. Then I convert these words into my mini-story.

I imagine myself struggling to carry an immense, 10 foot high version of my bank card. Suddenly a big door with a huge brass knocker opens in the side of the bank card. Through the doorway comes an vast purple, bulgy tree, growing at immense speed like something out of a science fiction movie. (Did you see *Evolution*? That should give you the idea.) It stretches up higher and higher until the clouds get caught in its branches. Finally, a great big, red high-heeled shoe comes down out of the cloud and squashes the tree with a loud squelch.

Notice a couple of details in my example. Things are big, dramatic and more than a little strange. That all helps fix them in memory. We remember the extraordinary. And though it's mostly literal (and I could have used any of the 'heaven' imagery you are likely to meet in a cartoon or a movie), there's no problem using sky or clouds for heaven as long as you have that well fixed in mind.

That story worked for me. The first few times I need to get the number back I have to reconstruct the story, replaying the visuals in my mind as the number is assembled. A door opened in the card (door = 4), then a tree came out (tree = 3, so that's 43), it reached up to heaven (heaven = 7, 437) and was squashed by a shoe (shoe = 2, 4372). Before long, the number will become so strongly associated with my credit card that I won't need to go through the story any more.

Try it now for a number you should know, but usually can't remember. It's probably better to start with a fairly short number and work up to something longer, like a phone number. Remember that this technique might not be 100 per cent reliable until you have those word/number rhymes absolutely fixed so you can instantly reply 'hen' to ten, for instance. (You could use 'hero' for zero if you prefer that to 'ten', as we're really remembering zero, but hens make better visuals – it's hard to spot a hero just from the mental picture.) Keep plugging away at remembering them. Within days they should be well on their way to being absolutely fixed in place, then you can amaze friends and relations with your ability to memorize numbers on the spot.

It is worth combining this technique with chunking for meaningful numbers. For instance, if the number had the string 999 or 911, the emergency numbers in the United Kingdom and United States respectively, then there's no need to fix line, line, line or line, gun, gun into your story – just build in the emergency services. Similarly, all the numbers in the village in which I live have the same area code, and the same first three digits. So, all I need to fix is the final three digits to pin down the phone number of anyone in my village, even though it's an 11-digit phone number.

Numbers have shapes too

If you feel you work better visually, try this alternative to number rhymes. Feel free to change the image used if you can think of something that works better for you. The important thing is that it's a shape that you can strongly associate with the number. Mostly the ones I've used are based on the shape of the number itself:

1	– flag pole (or the sort of flag used on a golf course)
2	– swan
3	– a person's bottom (on its side)
4	– folding stool (falling over)
5	– cup (on its side)
6	– cherry
7	– scythe
8	– bow (tie)
9	– balloon
10 (hence 0)	– Laurel and Hardy

The use of these pictorial images is much the same as with the number rhymes, and again takes practice – probably a little more so to really connect the images to the numbers. As before, when you want to remember a number, make up a short story in your mind linking the context of the number (e.g. the person whose phone number it is) with the objects in the number shapes in the right order. Make the story as vivid and pictorial as you can. Go through the story a number of times to reinforce it.

Depending on the way your mind works, you may find that this technique works either better or worse than using number rhymes. Try both out several times after you have firmly lodged the key words and images in your memory. See which seems more natural and easy. I personally prefer the rhymes, but that might reflect a natural preference for words; others find the images simpler.

I want to tell you a story

Stories are useful well beyond just committing numbers to memory; they are also great for memorizing lists. There's a very simple party game in which a story technique can make you an absolute champion. I happened to play this game shortly after I first came across memory techniques and amazed everyone with how effortlessly I beat them. The game goes something like this. Everyone sits in a circle. The first person says, 'I have a bag, and in my bag I have a . . .' then thinks of something. Anything. So they might say 'And in my bag I have a duck.' Then the next person repeats what the previous person says and adds another item. 'I have a bag, and in my bag I have a duck and a pair of scissors.' On to the next person. 'I have a bag, and in my bag I have a duck, a pair of scissors and a red pen.'

As the game continues, the list of things in the bag gets longer and longer until someone can't remember and they are knocked out. Using a story-based technique, I was finding it trivial to keep lists of 30 or more things in mind. The approach is similar to that with the number rhymes, but here it's the actual objects in the list that are worked into the story. In the game above, my story would start with a cute little cartoon-style duck, waddling alongside the stream when a great, crocodile-like pair of scissors leaps out of the stream and tries to cut the duck in half. The duck grabs a pen and writes in large, blood-dripping writing, 'BEWARE OF THE DUCK' . . . or whatever.

It might seem difficult to commit 30 items or more to memory this way, but in fact the game's structure helps. Each time another person recites their list you don't just add a bit to the end of the story, but go through the whole story in your mind. That builds in natural recaps, making it easier to hold a complex story in place. This recapping method is an approach that can be helpful when remembering a list of things too.

As with the number rhyme lists, make your little story as visual, colourful, dramatic and all those other things as you can. It all helps.

Your brain in chains

The whole idea of linking together things to remember items as part of a story plays on the way your brain makes chains of associations. One handy way to make use of this tendency is to use a memory chain that already exists in your brain and fit your new information into it. This was the ancient Greek technique I mentioned earlier, which is quite sophisticated, considering it's over two thousand years old.

To use this approach, dig up some well-known, well-used chains in your memory. Popular ones include familiar journeys and well-remembered places. Sit in a quiet place, close your eyes and think yourself along the journey, or take a mental tour of the familiar place (a room in your house, perhaps). You need to be able to take that visual journey in your mind for this technique to work. Then take each of things on your list to remember, and place them at memorable places along your route, or put them clearly in locations around the room. (In your mind, that is.)

This way, the things you are trying to remember will piggyback on to the memory chain that is already in place. Still use the familiar approach – make the things to remember dramatic, colourful, noticeable versions of themselves, and fix them in place in your memory along the way of your journey, or around the room, or whatever other existing memory chain you are using. Before long, the things you are trying to remember will be fixed in place.

Do it out loud, write it, draw it

These techniques are great, but they aren't applicable to everything you have to remember. They will work for numbers or shopping lists or, with a bit of manipulation, historical dates or scientific equations. But they aren't so helpful when it comes to learning a script for a play, or the words of a presentation you want to give slickly, rather than reading word for word from a piece of paper.

Almost everyone has to do a presentation at some time. It might be a talk you have to give to a class at school, or a speech as part of a special occasion, or it could be something you need to do in your job in later life. I do a lot of public lectures on science subjects, and wherever that talk is given, whether it's in a village hall or a school or the Royal Institution in London, I want to make it interesting. There's nothing duller than someone reading a speech word for word from a script, head down, not looking at the audience. And though autocues are very good, most can't afford them, and all but the most expert autocue reader – someone like a newsreader on TV – can't help but sound artificial when reading from them. I have a number of useful tips to help with memory when giving a presentation.

The first essential is to lay your script out well on paper. I prefer to use a rather bigger font than I would for a normal written document. Break it up into short segments that reflect the natural flow of the talk – no more than two or three paragraphs long, usually. Give each segment a heading that stands out from the text. This should summarize what is in the section in a few keywords.

Once you are happy with the layout, read it through aloud, more than once – ideally at least four or five times. It might make you feel stupid, but it will give you the chance to change things that don't sound right, and it will start to fix the words in your memory. Reading aloud requires more brain activity than reading to yourself, and always helps to anchor material in your head (even if you aren't going to say it aloud in the end). Do stop and make changes the first time through – you will find phrases that looked great on paper but sound really clumsy when spoken – but after that, try to get through the whole thing in one go, as you will when you give the presentation for real.

Once you have read it through a couple of times, on the next pass try to do it mostly just from the headings. Don't read every word, just glance down, check the heading and keep on talking, looking straight ahead. When I first started doing presentations, I eventually got rid of the text and just worked from the headings. Now I find it better to keep the whole text, just in case I forget a detail and need to dig in. But for most presentations, after maybe three or four read-throughs I can go for several pages without even looking at the notes, and then only glance at the headings to make sure I haven't missed anything.

A great help for the memory is a PowerPoint show or similar presentation. Some people moan about PowerPoint presentations, but that's just because they see so many bad ones. The important thing is that the slides should add material (visuals, etc.) to your speech, and should have relatively few keywords that sum up what you are saying, rather than having lots of text that repeats what you say word for word. Never read from a PowerPoint presentation; that's deadly dull. But just as those keywords help your audience fix what you've said in their minds, they also help you to remember where you are up to, and what comes next.

You still need to do all the rest – a full script, keyword headings, reading it through several times – with a PowerPoint show. Don't think that just because you've put together a PowerPoint you can speak from it without preparing the words. The result will be terrible. You may think really good speakers don't use scripts. It's more that they don't stick to them. When you are really confident with your script, you can ad lib, putting in extra things that occur to you, reacting to your audience as you go, but if you don't have a script at all you will probably flounder.

Acting in a play, or other situations where you have to remember text and recite it back, as much as possible word perfect, is really just a variant of the exercise where you lose the notes entirely. It's still important to read your part through aloud as you memorize it. Then, as you get to act with others, use their lines, their actions, what you see around you, to help fix what you have to say and do in your mind. You haven't got a PowerPoint presentation to prompt you, but you do have the other actors, props and scenery to act as mental hooks on which to hang all that dialogue that will seem impossible to remember at the start, but will eventually become second nature.

I know the face, but what's the name?

Perhaps the most common memory weakness is being able to remember people's names. I've lost count of the number of people I've heard say, 'I'm terrible with names', or 'I'm good with faces, but I can never remember names.' Luckily, very similar techniques to those used to commit numbers and lists to memory can also be make names much easier to remember.

Let me give you a real example. When I first learned memory techniques, which was many, many years ago, I was really impressed with the name thing, because, yes, I am terrible with names. So I went out to a nearby shopping mall and went into a shop (it was Boots, if you're interested) and looked at the name badge of the person behind the counter. She was called Ann Hibble. I have never seen the name anywhere since – but it got so firmly embedded in my memory that I can still remember it today.

Committing names to memory is just like that game of 'in my bag I have . . .', except that you've usually only a couple of words to deal with. Take my shop assistant. I fixed a picture of where she worked in my mind. I imagined a great big hippopotamus looming out of the floor as if out of a great river, and nibbling the shop assistant's toes. So, **an hi**ppo was **ni**bb**ling** her toes. An hippo nibbling. Ann Hibble. OK, it's really weak and I had to mess around with the words to make it work. Yet it has stuck with me all these years.

Usually you don't have to resort to such complicated chopping up; it's just what occurred to me and worked for me visually. A lot of surnames mean something, so you can use the word as part of your picture. Traditional first names are a little harder. Although a modern name with an association like Chelsea isn't such a problem if you know the place or the football team, a name like Rebecca is harder to deal with. The way I normally deal with difficult first names is to use a person I already know well with that name in my imagery. It might be a friend, or a famous person – as long as I have a clear picture of a Rebecca, I can use that person in putting my picture together.

Surnames are often easier. A surname may be the name of something or sound like something – so I have no problem remembering the name of someone I know whose surname is Mudd, especially as he is very fastidious kind of person, who is unlikely to be seen with muddy clothes. If you get a name like McDonald, which doesn't conjure up a direct picture (what does a McDonald look like?), you can either use an association – very few people would have to look far for an association with McDonald – or you can break it up, so I could imagine a cartoon-style duck wearing a kilt and playing the bagpipes.

Once there's a clear picture in your mind, you can link that to the actual person. Think about the image while looking at the person. Incorporate that person into the image. Include any special characteristics they have – things about them that make them unique – and link them to the name image. Ideally, as you are looking at the person, say the person's name aloud as often as you can, though this can make you look very silly in some circumstances.

You can just imagine it. 'Hello, David Smith, it's so nice to meet you, David Smith. I'm not sure I've ever met someone called David Smith before. Davids, yes. And Smiths. But not a David Smith.' It oozes with embarrassment. But it's quite common to use someone else's name just after meeting them. Make the most of it to help embed the name in memory, combining the repetition with your mental images.

This sounds a lengthy process, but can be done in seconds with practice. You need never forget a name again.

Recap and recap . . . and recap again

Given that I can remember the name of Ann Hibble from so long ago, you may expect that I can remember everything I've ever used a memory technique to force into memory. In fact, you might think I can remember the name of everyone I've ever met. Well, no. It doesn't work like that. The memory technique helps establish something in long-term memory, but, rather like a flowerbed, that memory needs regular nurturing to stay healthy. It's time for a recap.

The reason I can still instantly think of Ann Hibble is not just that I used a memory technique to fix her name, but also that I've referred to it regularly over the years. About six months ago I used the same technique on someone's name . . . but I can't remember what they were called. I've a faint idea that her first name was something like Melanie, and I know the second name was one that could be singular or plural, but I can't bring it back. (I've just checked and she was called Natasha, which shows how wrong you can be.) I regularly refer to Ann Hibble, unlike Natasha, when I give talks on memory techniques, which means her name has been constantly refreshed in my memory.

Aside: Self-patterning systems

The brain's information store is a self-patterning system. This sounds more complicated than it is. It just means that the more you use a connection, the easier it becomes to use. The less you use it, the fainter it gets and the less likely you are to remember it. A physical example of a self-patterning system is a board covered with a thick layer of wax. Imagine holding the board at an angle and pouring a thin stream of hot water on to the top of the board, so it runs down the wax-coated side. To begin with, the stream of water will wander randomly, but soon it will melt a channel in the wax. Once the channel is there, the hot water will tend to use that channel, so the channel will get bigger. The only difference with the brain is that if you stop using the channel it will gradually fill back up with mental 'wax' until it disappears and the memory (or rather your access path to the memory) has gone.

It's quite possible the memory is still there, but you just can't reach it. This is why you can recall something you had totally forgotten at a later date. It's also why it's easier to remember things if you aren't under pressure. If you stop trying to remember, it will often come back to you. This is because under pressure (see page 10) your brain uses thick, frequently used connections. It's only when you aren't pushing things that it can meander down infrequently used paths and hit that missing memory.

Recapping is not good news. To be honest, it's deeply boring. It's about going over the material again and again, refreshing your memory – yes, it's revision. But the way most of us revise for examinations, leaving everything until the last couple of weeks, is not a good way to recap to make sure something is firmly fixed in memory. To really make sure a piece of information stays available, I'd recommend recapping after an hour if possible (not always easy, that one), then a day later, a week, a month and around six months. Realistically, this means putting entries in your diary to remind you to recap if you really want to remember something, which sounds weird, but it works. If you are revising the content of a book, you can usually recap from a summary; you don't need to read the whole thing again, as long as the summary has all the key points.

Once you have done four to five recaps over gradually increasing periods of time, the chances are it will be with you for ever. I can go for years without thinking about Ann Hibble, but she (and her hippopotamus) still pop back into my mind at a moment's notice. Recapping may be tedious, but it works.

Will I run out of space?

One concern some people have when learning how to memorize things is that are they going to fill up their mental storage to the extent that they won't be able to remember anything at all after a while. This is computer thinking, not brain thinking. Remember, there are many more potential ways of connecting up the neurons in the brain than there are atoms in the universe. (That's not to say that each combination is like a different memory 'bit', again that's too computer-like.)

There is no evidence that you will ever run out of space. Just keep piling things in; there's plenty of room up there.

The 'can't be bothered' phenomenon

There is one feature of memory techniques I really can't explain. It's true of all creativity techniques to some extent, but comes out more in memory techniques than any other. For some reason, there is a strong 'can't be bothered' reaction even when you know the techniques perfectly well and know how well they work. Although I could memorize the name of everyone I'm introduced to, I hardly ever use a memory technique to do so.

The only times I normally use these techniques is if I've a meeting with someone I want to impress, when I'll make sure I know their name using a technique, or, if I need a phone number, when it's so useful I can't not use a technique. Otherwise I tend not to bother. I suppose I think, 'I don't really need to remember people's names, no one else can, so why should I bother?'

This is downright dumb. It really is incredibly easy to use these techniques – and the more you use them, the easier it becomes. Don't succumb to 'can't be bothered'. Keep using the techniques, especially when you have something important to remember.

Memories are made of this – essentials

OK, time for your first recap (but remember to come back again!):

- Brains aren't computers – we store memories as links and chains with plenty of visual input, not as bits.
- Break numbers down into recognizable chunks to remember them.
- Learn and use the number rhymes (1 – gun, 2 – shoe, 3 – tree, 4 – door, 5 – hive, 6 – sticks, 7 – heaven, 8 – weight, 9 – line, 10 (0) – hen).
- Make lists into little stories. Make the images in the story dramatic, colourful, rude and exaggerated to force the story into memory.

- When giving presentations, practise out loud and write out your material broken into chunks with keyword summaries.
- Use dramatic visual imagery to remember names. If the name has no image in your mind, use associations – people you know, celebrities, etc.
- Recap after about an hour (if possible), a day, a week, a month and six months to a year.

Chapter 6

Read for speed

Can you remember when you learned to read? It was probably a long, long time ago. Over time, you will have got more confident, though you might still find that reading aloud without a chance to practise can be difficult. Reading is something very few of us take past the basics. There's no advanced reading course at high school; it's assumed you learned to read by the time you're about 10 and after that you just get on and use that ability. Yet reading is something that is central to studying. If you can learn to read better (we'll worry about what 'better' means when it comes to reading in a minute) then you will be able to study better. No question. Reading is absolutely central to studying – so let's make things better.

Back to basics

One obvious type of 'better' is if you can read faster. You won't want to read *everything* faster. If you've a book you are really enjoying, or you need to get every last drop of meaning out a book, you might want to read more slowly (and this technique will work for that as well), but often when studying you need to get through a piece of text quickly to pick out one or two facts. There's nothing more subject to fads and new ideas than the ways small children are taught to read, so you might not have begun with a finger on the page, pointing to the word to be read – but lots of people did, and we'll be returning to something like that pointing finger for this exercise.

To speed up your reading you need a visual guide, something to give your eyes a cue. This is because, thanks to your brilliant brain, you don't realize just how wayward your eyes are. Even when you think you are looking steadily at something, your eyes are making tiny, very quick movements called saccades. The brain edits these out to give you a steady view. That's a bit frightening when you think about it. What you 'see', the picture of the world you think is coming from your eyes, isn't really what your eyes pick up. Your eyes aren't like video cameras; instead, your brain assembles a picture from information from various different visual modules like ones that handle shapes or movement. (This is why you can see movies as moving pictures, rather than a series of still pictures. It has nothing to do with 'persistence of vision'; this was a mistake from the Victorian era that you still see in textbooks today.)

Faced with a whole page (or more often the two facing pages) of a book, your eyes are naturally flitting around here and there, limiting your ability to read word by word along a sentence. But put in a visual guide – something that directs your eyes where to focus – and you can speed up the whole reading process. You can still use a finger, but many readers find using the end of a pen or pencil easier (or less embarrassing). Try both, and see which feels better.

To begin with, just read normally, but trace under the words as you read them with your guide. You will probably feel a bit stupid, because it looks very childish to be reading following a finger or pencil, so it's best to do this somewhere on your own. Gradually – very gradually – build up the speed at which you move the pointer. You will find with a few minutes' practice that you can speed up noticeably, and after a few hours you will probably be able to double your reading speed while still taking in all the information. Obviously there will be a limit to the speed at which you can take things in, but keep trying until you have a comfortable, but noticeably faster, speed.

When you are happy with using the guide, there's another way of using it that can give you even faster reading speed. Start with the guide (your finger or pencil or pen) at the top of the page, in the middle. Now bring the guide slowly down the page. As you do, let your eyes flick along the line, but keep coming back to the guide. This approach takes more practice, and you may always find that you miss a few words, but with time you will be able to skim-read a page using the central guide even faster than using a word-by-word guide that travels along each line. It does take a while to get used to this second technique; don't give up if it doesn't work initially.

Some people find with time that they can eventually drop the guide and keep the speed. Others will always need the guide to keep their eyes on track. Find what works best for you – but with an afternoon's practice, you should be able to push up your reading speed significantly, when you want to read quickly (remember, that's not all the time).

In a flash

You've probably seen science fiction movies in which some superhero or robot picks up a book and reads it by flicking through it, taking seconds or less on each page. One further technique that can help with your reading speed is rather like this. It sounds impossible, but it's worth trying.

Take a book and begin to 'read' it – but only allow yourself around two seconds for each page. If you have a metronome, or something that will give a regular tick, use that to guide you. Otherwise just give yourself what feels like a couple of seconds. To begin with, just let your eyes drift over the page without your making any conscious effort to take anything in. After a number of pages, really try to take in what is on the page as you scan it.

This technique may seem bizarre, but it does two good things. It's not really supposed to let you read books at this speed, though you may find with practice that you can take in a surprising amount. Instead, it's a way of getting your brain used to handling the effects of high-speed reading, so that when you read at a more normal speed it seems trivial to take things in. It's a bit like when you've been driving on a high-speed road for a long time, then get back on to an ordinary road. The speed your car goes seems much slower than normal on the normal road, because you've got used to moving quickly. In the same way, a high-speed pass through the pages of a book can make even a fast normal reading speed seem manageable.

While it's possible that this technique will help you take in information at the two seconds per page rate, the main idea here is that after few sessions of this speed scanning, you should be able to speed up your normal reading even further. Like using a reading guide, this can both increase the amount of information you can absorb in a given time and give you more time to absorb what you are reading and make something of it.

Sinking in

Strangely, although we've so far concentrated on speeding up your reading, there are some things you can do to make your reading more effective that involve slowing down. Some information – in textbooks, for instance – can be so badly written that you need to take things slowly just to understand what is being said. In that case, you might find you naturally skip parts of the text. Before long you're totally lost, you don't get the point and you have to go back and read it all over again.

If that is happening, you can speed up by slowing down. (It's one of those irritating 'more haste less speed' things.) Again, using a guide like your finger or a pencil can really help where you are having trouble absorbing the information, just by slowing down your pace, and keeping your eyes in place rather than letting them skip ahead.

Another really valuable tool in helping things sink in is note taking as you go. As we saw in Chapter 4, note-taking techniques like mind mapping can be used quickly and flexibly. Jotting down key notes as you read will make the information sink in much faster than reading the whole thing, then trying to take notes afterwards. You will have problems keeping all that you need in memory if you try to store it all up. But taking notes as you go, fishing out the key facts, will help your brain to structure and absorb the information.

Screening your work

These days, a lot of our reading is done from screens. As I edit this text at the moment, I am reading it direct from the screen, rather than printing it out on paper first. This isn't a bad thing, but you need to be aware of some limitations. First of all, screens might be very good these days, but they still aren't anywhere near the resolution of a printed piece of paper. This means your eyes get tired sooner, and you are more likely to miss things. They also limit just how you can read: it has to be either sitting up at your desk, or with your laptop perched somewhere.

There's nothing wrong with doing basic research direct on the web. And it's fine for taking a quick overview of a longer piece of text. But to absorb it in detail it's much better to get hold of it in printed form, either in a book or by printing it off from your computer.

This particularly applies if the thing you are reading is your own work. All the professionals whose job is proof reading – looking for mistakes in print – and copy editing – improving the presentation and language of a written piece – will tell you that they need to use a printed copy to really see what needs changing. The same goes for your work. It's fine to do a first pass on the screen, but it's best if you can do the final polishing on paper. However many times you go through it on the screen, the chances are that you will find something else that needs changing when it's on paper . . . and you can read it where you like, somewhere comfortable, which can also help.

You may wonder, given this fact, why I'm editing on screen. That's because at this stage I'm still making significant changes, so it's much easier to work directly on the computer. But later on in the book-writing process I will sit down with a printed copy of the book (in a comfy chair, rather than at my desk), and read it through looking for mistakes. Both techniques are valuable, but it's easy not to bother with the printed version unless you realize how helpful it can be.

Hunting for essentials

Probably the hardest skill to learn when it comes to improving your reading is the ability to skim through a book and pick out the essentials. If you are reading a book to enjoy it, or to get an appreciation of the whole of a book that you will have to write a report on later, you need to read it word for word. But with a lot of non-fiction texts you are trying to suck out the essential juices without bothering with all the padding.

Perhaps I'm being a little harsh, calling the less important text 'padding', but it's certainly true that lots of the words in a book aren't really necessary to get across the key essentials. I've written a book on time management (*Instant Time Management*) which runs to about 50,000 words, and I've seen weighty time management tomes that are twice that length (though I don't know who has time to read them). I have also contributed to a series called Crazy Colour Cards, which put everything you need to know about a subject on two sides of a laminated card, similar in area to two sides of A4 or letter paper. The card I wrote on time management, which can't contain more than around 800 words, has everything you really need to know to do time management effectively.

So why bother to write a full-length book at all? In part it's simple economics. Even if that card does contain everything a full-price book does, no one is going to pay as much for a laminated card as for a book. And the card is a very different way of presenting the information that doesn't work for everyone. Also, there are many things in the book, like exercises, that are very valuable but couldn't have been included in the card. The fact is, when you are trying to communicate a subject, a book gives you the chance to include so much more, and to put the message across in a much more detailed fashion.

Even so, you will often want to strip out those non-essentials, and there are a few tips and tricks along the way that can help. First, look out for summaries. A lot of technical, educational and business books have a summary at the end of each chapter. (This reflects an old teacher's saying, 'tell them what you are going to tell them, tell them, then tell them what you told them', because recapping (as we saw in the memory chapter) is a very practical technique if you are going to remember anything. In this book the chapters end with an 'essentials' section, which gives a good example of what I mean. If your intention in reading is to pick out a few key pieces of information, then by skimming through and reading these summaries first you can take in the basics and know where best to concentrate your reading effort.

Even if there aren't specific summary sections, you can often pick up a lot of what's in a chapter of a book by reading the first few paragraphs and the last few. There's a natural temptation to sum up at the end of a chapter. Losing the middle of a chapter doesn't always work, but often does. This technique is also very helpful if you are trying to see whether an article or academic paper is going to be helpful. With these, there is usually a summary up front (often called the abstract). Read that, the first couple of paragraphs and the last couple of paragraphs (where this is usually a conclusion), and you can get a feel for the whole article. Again this isn't a substitute for reading it all the way through, but if you have hundreds of articles in front of you and you only want to extract a smallish amount of information, it beats reading them all end to end and should make it obvious which articles you need to study in more detail.

With books you may also find that the introduction or preface summarizes the whole content. Introductions are odd things, which many people skip, as they can be quite dull. Sometimes they just give the writer a chance to say why they wrote the book and what it means to them. Others give a brief introduction to the subject, if it's an obscure one. Yet another kind, bizarrely, are written by someone else. These tend to be contributed by a famous person or an academic, which is usually something the publisher forces on the author in attempt to push up sales. (At the most extreme, the name of the person who wrote the introduction will be bigger than the author's name on the cover. That's when you know a publisher is desperate.) But some introductions summarize the book chapter by chapter. They are a pain if you intend to read the book cover to cover, and should then be avoided at all costs, but they are great if you want to get an overview and just dip in to the parts that interest you.

A final tip: if you have done the speed reading exercises, you should be quite good by now at skimming through a book and getting the general idea, even if you aren't picking it up word for word. To extend this technique to hunting for essentials, be aware of some key words that you are looking for to help with the information you need. Skim through, looking for those key words. When your practised eye spots them, slow down and read a couple of paragraphs either side. This way you can quickly home in on the right parts you need to read.

Read for speed – essentials

- Start with a reading guide – a finger or pen or pencil – that you move along the words as you read.
- Gradually speed up the guide to increase your reading speed.
- Try dropping the guide once you are comfortable – but be prepared to reinstate it.
- Try moving the guide down the middle of the page for a faster skim-read.
- Try taking in what you can at two seconds per page. Even though you can't really read this way, it will improve your normal reading speed.
- Use note taking and slowing down where necessary to take things in thoroughly.
- To read something in depth, print it off rather than reading from a computer screen.
- Use summaries, first and last parts, introductions and skim-reading to pick out essentials.
- Look out for key words in a text and read a paragraph or two either side of them.

Chapter 7

Chill out

Being creative isn't something that you can always turn on like a tap. It works better at some times and in some places than it does in others. In the next chapter we'll look at how to handle your time in order to be creative. This one is more about getting your brain working more effectively by dealing with your environment.

My brain time

We've already looked at some ways in which the human brain is different from a computer. Here's another one: it doesn't work as well at every single time of day. Sometimes it's sluggish. At other times it's firing on all cylinders and ready to take on the world. (Actually, my computer is a bit like that too, but it *shouldn't* be.)

A typical picture of how a brain has its ups and downs during the day is shown opposite.

I've made up a measure of how well your brain is working called the *With-it index*. At 100 per cent your brain is absolutely working at its best. At 0 per cent you are unconscious. The graph is roughly my own. The positioning of the bars will differ from person to person – you'll probably have friends who are irritatingly bright first thing, or keep going until the early hours of the morning when you just want to crash out – but everyone has similar basic features. I'll just pick out the highlights.

Soon after waking up, practically everyone is totally hopeless. You really shouldn't do anything requiring serious brain input, and particularly should avoid anything risky (driving, for instance), for at least half an hour after waking up. Your brain gets into gear slowly. Gradually, depending on how much of a morning person you are, your brain revs up to a peak of full working efficiency. But after a while, it

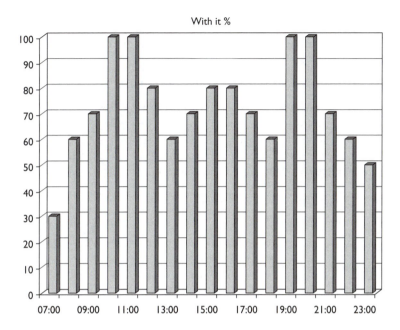

With it %

all gets too much. Late morning, it's not unusual for concentration to start to lapse. Then you have a meal, and there's a real dip as the body concentrates more of its efforts on your stomach.

You will probably never hit quite the same highs in the afternoon, before things drop off again towards the end of the afternoon and you are hit by another meal. Then, though, typically, another peak comes along. By early evening you are refreshed and ready to use your brain again, before its performance gradually slides away as you get more and more tired.

Knowing this, if you want to get the most out of your brain, it's best to slot the work that needs creative input in at your peak times. Often, mid-morning is best, followed by early evening, and then early afternoon, once you've recovered from lunch. The exact distribution of your With-it index will vary a bit from my example. Why not plot out your own With-it index, then use that as a guide? Stick in the undemanding, low brain activity work when your brain is in one of its troughs (some might be so low that you aren't capable of doing much more than watching a soap opera). Keep the creative work for your highs.

It makes sense. Why pretend that your brain works the same all through the day? It doesn't – and by making use of your With-it index, you can make the best of your brain's highs and lows.

Where and when am I creative?

When I'm not writing books I spend my time teaching people – usually business people – about creativity. Over the years I've asked hundreds of people in what circumstances they have their ideas. They have come up with all sorts of suggestions, some of them too rude to repeat. Here are a few of the most common:

- In the bath
- At the gym
- Bouncing ideas off other people
- Walking
- On the toilet
- Daydreaming
- In the bath
- Gardening
- In bed
- Playing
- On the train
- In the shower
- In the country
- Driving my car

What hardly anyone ever says is 'sitting at my desk', and *no one* says 'under pressure'. I'll come back to that pressure bit later, but let's work on the 'sitting at my desk' problem. OK, these are business-people, but creativity is creativity – it really doesn't matter what you want to do with it, the circumstances that help the creativity flow are the same.

Part of the problem with being creative at your desk is the distractions. For businesspeople it's the office noise and the phones and the bustle around them. For you it might be the other people around, or the temptation to do something different. We'll look at that more in the next chapter. But there's also the fact that you have to be really lucky to have a desk where it's nice to be.

Often you've a rather uncomfortable chair, a cluttered desk full of junk (and quite possibly the remains of yesterday's snack), no view and little room to move. Look at that list above. A lot of it involves getting away from the desk. Sometimes that's an essential. Next time you have to come up with a new idea, give it a try. Give yourself a few minutes somewhere else – your equivalent of those thinking places in the list. Somewhere you can really let your brain roam free. Take a way of making notes with you. If it's a place you are sitting with your hands free, a simple notepad will do. Otherwise, take some sort of voice recorder (some phones, MP3 players and PDAs have a voice memo facility) and capture your thoughts that way.

You can't always work that way, though. You will still have to do some of your work at your desk. So for those times, put a bit of effort into making your desk a cool place to be. Get yourself two sheets of paper. On one sheet, list everything that's wrong with your desk and the room it's in as a place to be creative. On the other, list anything that you feel the ideal desk and working environment should have. Now pull the two together. What can you do to get rid of the nasties, and to bring more of the ideal into the place you work? Some of it you could do straight away – so why not do it now? Some of it will take time or money. Look for the opportunities to make small or cheap changes that can make a lot of difference. It's amazing how much you can alter the feel of a place with a few small changes.

Balancing pressure

What about the 'under pressure' part in saying that people aren't creative under pressure or at their desk? One thing we need to get straight up front. When I say 'under pressure', this doesn't refer to having to meet a sensible deadline, like 'I've an essay to hand in on Monday morning', at least unless it's Sunday night already and you haven't started on it. All the evidence is that having deadlines, especially perhaps ones that stretch you a little, helps to get the ideas flowing. Stress itself isn't a bad thing. Good stress is what drives us to achieve, to aim for something new. But a lot of the pressure we're all under isn't so helpful. If you are wound up, stressed, tense, worried – it can all flatten creativity.

There's a good reason for this. If you look at the list in the previous section of 'how and when' people get creative, they are often situations where you can get into a bit of a daydream state. And that's when ideas come easiest.

Your brain has four main modes of operation. In sleep it is operating very slowly, and can make the connections that are necessary for ideas with frightening ease – but usually the sleep state isn't very useful, because you can't point your thinking in a particular direction, and your brain's internal censors aren't operating, so it can't tell an idea from a random set of garbage.

In the daydream state, things are cycling a little quicker in the brain's processing, but it's still pretty easy to make new connections. Ideas seem to flow easily. Yet your mind is active enough to control what's going on. It's ideal.

Aside: Daydreaming in a car

I don't actually recommend daydreaming while driving a car (it doesn't matter, of course, if you're a passenger), even though this is one of the items on the list. Even so, a lot of people driving on a familiar road do experience a sudden shock when they realize they've travelled for several minutes without the faintest idea of how they got there. This is the daydream state in action – but it can be dangerous, and shouldn't be attempted intentionally.

To be able to get into a daydream state while driving, the process of handling the car has to come automatically. This only tends to happen to experienced drivers. Doing any repetitive task that you can undertake and simultaneously let your mind wander (some people swear by knitting, for example, though I can't comment from experience) can be quite effective for releasing the daydream state.

Most of the time we are awake we are out of the daydream state, fully conscious. Now it's that bit harder to make new connections. As the brain cycles more and more quickly, the tendency is to use well-trodden paths, to go with the existing way of doing things and not to come up with anything new. The more the pressure increases, the less chance there is of coming up with an idea. Eventually, as panic sets in, the brain begins to churn, going round and round in circles, losing the ability to think practically. At the extreme, it's the 'rabbits in the headlights' syndrome. Brain-freeze. No real thinking at all.

One important thing to realize is that it's much easier to switch up from daydream state to fully awake than it is to go the other way. We can all jump instantly out of the daydream state at the approach of a teacher, on hearing a shout, on being touched. Yet it's practically impossible to go straight into the daydream state. You can't command your brain to do it. It doesn't happen as an automatic response to a stimulus like a noise. And that's why the environment you do your thinking in is so important. It's so much easier to slip down a mental level if you are relaxed, comfortable and in a pleasant place.

Natural medication

Apart from simple speeding up of the brain as it tries to cope with pressure, there is another problem for creativity that is caused by stress. When you are stressed, your brain produces a range of chemicals – in effect, natural medication. Two types are of particular interest. One is adrenaline (known as epinephrine in the United States). This is a hormone, and acts as a neurotransmitter – one of the signalling chemicals of the brain. Adrenaline is released because your brain assumes that stress is connected to physical danger. Adrenaline increases the heart rate and prepares the body for fight or flight – for attacking or running away. Unfortunately, from a creative viewpoint this is not helpful, as the result is faster cycling of the brain and less ability to make new connections.

At the same time, the brain triggers the release of endorphins. The clue to what's going to happen here is the alternative name, endo-morphines. Like other opiates, these are painkillers, released into the system on the assumption that the outcome of that fight or flight could be physical harm to the body. Sadly, these too have a negative effect on thinking. They dull down your capacity to think at all.

All in all, being stressed isn't helpful for creativity. Luckily, dealing with stress isn't difficult if you know a few tricks of the trade. Here are ten easy ways to make sure that stress doesn't block your creativity.

Destress 1: Get some sleep and some good food

You only have to speak to someone who has had a baby for the first time to realize how stressful going without sleep can be. We're all conscious of the limited time there is to live a life, and want to squeeze every last drop out. If you're a student, you probably don't consider sleep one of your most important priorities. That's fine, but insufficient sleep is a sure-fire source of stress. (Apparently it also tends to make you fatter as well, but let's not worry about that.)

This exercise just involves spending a little while thinking about your sleeping and what you can do about it. If you have regular variations in sleep patterns of more than about an hour a day, you are likely to suffer. But it's one thing to prescribe sleep (and only you can determine how much you need, though for most people from their mid-teens it's about seven to eight hours), and it's another to get it.

There are mental and physical techniques to help. Make sure you aren't trying to remember something as you go to sleep. If something you need to do next day is nagging at you, jot it down, even if it means getting out of bed. Don't try to go to sleep straight after a passionate discussion; wind down first. If something is going round and round in your head, sit up and pin it down; don't try to force sleep on yourself. When you do lie down, use a calming, tranquil mental image to help drift into sleep. Some people find a warm, non-stimulating drink helps. Alternatively, try a warm bath, followed by getting straight into a warm bed – but make sure the bath isn't hot, as this will stimulate you rather than help you to wind down.

Sleep deprivation piles stress on stress until you are almost driven mad. If you aim for the sleep you need to feel well, rather than the sleep you can get away with, you are going to underpin all your other efforts in managing stress.

Then there's food. There's no magic link between food and stress relief, but being broadly healthy will help you deal with stress, and diet is a contributory factor to health. While there are constant arguments about some specifics of diet – do eggs increase cholesterol levels? Are vegetables better raw or boiled? – some aspects of dietary sense are very clear. The fact that most of us should reduce our intake of saturated fat and salt, while eating more vegetables, fruit, fish, fibre and (surprising to some, particularly those who've come across the Atkins diet) an appropriate amount of carbohydrates, is hard to dispute. Similarly, most of us ought to drink more water, especially if we are under stress when we are more likely to become dehydrated.

Spend a few minutes thinking about what you eat. Identify a handful of changes that would improve your diet. Think about how you could implement these changes. For example, if you wanted to eat more fruit and vegetables, could you have a carrot and an apple on your desk for when you get peckish? Often the reason we don't eat 'better' food is that it's too much trouble – so make good food easy instead. Similarly, keep a glass or a bottle of water with you when you are working. You will find you drink almost automatically because it's there. Keep topping it up regularly.

Being fussy about your diet can actually be stressful. Most of us don't find dieting particularly enjoyable, and at times it is a positive pain. If you love junk food, for instance, I'm not suggesting totally ignoring it; that will stress you. But you could cut back. Make the junk food a special treat, something to aim for when you've completed an important task, say once a week or once a fortnight.

Unless you have medical reasons for sticking to a diet, be prepared to break it infrequently but quite regularly like this as a treat, to celebrate and to unwind. Similarly, a regular if controlled amount of alcohol (if you aren't under age!), particularly red wine, isn't a bad idea unless you have associated medical problems. Although alcohol is actually a stimulant, many people find a small amount of alcoholic drink helpful in the process of unwinding. The problems caused by alcohol are usually down to drinking too much, particularly in one go. If you are over the legal age and keep the amount you drink low – say no more than a glass of wine or beer a day – alcohol isn't a problem for stress.

Destress 2: Get on top of your time

Stress is often caused by having too much to do in too little time. It's not just about having enough time, it's about breaking up what you do into manageable chunks so it doesn't get on top of you. I won't put anything specific here, as the next chapter is dedicated to taking control of your time, an essential if you are going to be creative.

Destress 3: Get some air

Breathing is good for you. OK, you probably knew that already. But your breathing is a great secret weapon for overcoming stress so you can get on with being creative. Not just any breathing, though – there's breathing and there's breathing. First, as all singers know, there are two *types* of breathing: with the chest muscles and with the diaphragm. The second type is more controlled and gives you a much deeper breath, yet it tends to be underused, particularly by those under stress.

First try to feel that breathing from the diaphragm. Stand up, straight but not tense. Take a deep breath and hold it for a second.

Your chest will rise. Now try to keep your chest in the 'up' position while breathing in and out. You should feel a tensing and relaxing of muscles around the stomach area. Rest a hand gently on your stomach to feel it in action.

Now lie on the floor or sit comfortably in a chair. Close your eyes. Begin to breathe regularly: count up to five (in your head!) as you breathe in through your nose. Hold it for a couple of seconds, then breathe out through your mouth, again counting to five. Rest a hand on your stomach. Don't consciously force your rib cage to stay up now, but concentrate on movement of the diaphragm. Your stomach should gently rise as you breathe in and fall as you breathe out.

One of the great things about breathing exercises like this is that they can be performed pretty well anywhere. For instance, although driving a car isn't the ideal position, you can still indulge in deep breathing (though don't close your eyes or lie down). You can even do this kind of exercise in a class with other people around you and they'll never realize you're doing it. A regular five-minute session of breathing properly will provide the foundation for many other stress management techniques. It is simple and very effective.

Destress 4: Get a laugh

It's easy for stress to cause more stress, which causes even more stress and so on, building up and up in a horrible spiral. The more stressed you are, the unhappier you become. A great way to break out of that spiral is laughter.

Make yourself a laughter first aid kit. Spend a couple of minutes jotting down things that make you laugh. It could be certain books, cartoons, movies, comedians, TV shows – or just a good evening out with your friends. Make sure you have some of your laughter triggers available, easy to get hold of, when you are really feeling stressed out.

If stress is getting you down, make an effort. Go out and see a comedian or a funny movie. Have a good time. To start with, taking action will seem artificial and unnatural. All the people enjoying themselves around you are likely to seem alien and strange, when you are unhappy. But it's very hard to resist for too long. We like joining in with laughter. It's much better than any pill for curing simple stress.

A related thing to do is to play. Play is a valuable way to ease stress very naturally. It's sad that we lose a lot of our ability to play as we grow up, when we need it in this respect more than ever. This exercise is not about playing sporting games – in fact, most sport isn't play at all, in the sense of being fun and unstructured.

Find some form of play in which you can totally lose yourself. It might be playing PC games or board games or silly party games. It might be conjuring up a fantasy world as you sit on the subway train, or trying not to step on the cracks in the pavement, or even saying 'boing' every time you pass someone with red hair. Just play. Such play can be undertaken at pretty well any time of day (especially the types of play that don't involve technology) and can last a few minutes or hours. The great thing about play is that not only are you putting aside all your everyday stressors, but the activity you are involved in is deliberately not important. It doesn't matter what happens, it is just play.

Some people find it difficult to see how playing a computer game fits with this picture. The right sort of game is an excellent candidate. It has to be something you enjoy and, most importantly, for a single player. Yes, you can get involved, even excited, while playing such a game, but underneath you know it does not matter in the slightest. This is why this is a very different technique to sport, which is valuable as physical exercise but can provide a stress of its own because the outcome is more important. Again, multiplayer games are not so effective because other people depend on you and can see how you perform. Don't think that play's just for little kids; we all need it.

Destress 5: Get physical

There's no doubt at all that physical exercise is a good remedy for stress – and it doesn't have to be a matter of hitting a punchbag pretending it's a person who is causing you grief. This is fine if you're one of those healthy types who are always out doing sports anyway, but not so good for the rest of us. If you tend to avoid exercise, give yourself some motivation.

Find reasons for doing the exercise – not just to reduce stress, but to get fit, to become more attractive to the opposite sex, to live longer, and so on. How could you not exercise with all that going for it? Then try to find something you are going to enjoy as a way to get that exercise. This may seem pretty obvious, but many people choose their form of exercise because it's trendy (the gym) or it's career boosting (golf), rather than because it's something they genuinely find fun. It might not be possible – you might hate all exercise – but try different activities in case one really works for you. Even if you don't like doing the exercise, you can make it more acceptable by not just doing the exercise for its own sake. Get together with friends and make it a social event, or choose an activity where you can carry an MP3 player and listen to music or speech radio or audio books or learn a language. Or just combine the exercise with things you have to do anyway. Jog to the supermarket or to the post office.

Your activity should be aerobic, maximizing use of the body. Typical choices are swimming, cycling, running or gym routines; avoid sports like golf that don't involve continuous activity. If, like me, you find a session at the gym intensely boring, don't ignore walking. We're used to walking as a gentle stroll to introduce you to exercise. In fact, walking at high speed can be an effective exercise (especially if hills are involved) with less risk of damage than jogging. Walking is also a less efficient form of transport than using a bike, so you use up more energy – the point of exercise – than if you take up cycling. What's more, walking is practical. I hate exercise for its own sake; having the goal of getting somewhere doubles the value. Be warned, though. Plunging into heavy exercise is not good, particularly if you aren't very fit. Get some guidance if you are in any doubt.

Exercise reduces physical tension and brings down levels of stress chemicals. It also builds up the body, helping general fitness and ability to cope. The physical control of stress is the foundation on which everything else is built. You shouldn't overlook this one.

Destress 6: Get a winner's trophy

This sounds like something out of one of those ancient 1950s self-help books ('How I learned to conquer stress and realize I was a winner'). But it's not as feeble as it seems. Stress is very strongly linked to what you think about yourself. Studies have been done of people in different jobs. It turns out that it's not how 'stressful' the job appears to be that gives people trouble, it's how much control they have over what they do, and what they think of themselves.

The simplest way to build up self-esteem is to recognize that you've succeeded at something. You can do this two ways. One is by recognizing your own little achievements. Every day you will succeed at something – probably quite a lot of things. It might just be 'I got to a lecture on time' or 'I ate healthily today' or 'I managed to ask that person out for a date'. If you are feeling stressed, it's easy to ignore these achievements. Don't. Consciously think about the things you got right today. Over the next week, make a note of all your little achievements. It's amazing how helpful success can be in dealing with stress linked to low self-esteem.

The other approach (which should be used as well as, not instead of, the first one) is to be aware of your big achievements. Think back over your life so far. Note down any big achievements, from exam successes to climbing a mountain, from getting a driving licence to winning a race. Think back to that moment when you realized you'd done it. Just enjoy that sense of achievement. You did that. You deserve to feel positive.

Just using the memory of those past successes can help suppress stress. Even more so, make it a big deal in the future when you achieve big goals that you might have at the moment. Really celebrate – make it a success to remember, then use that memory later on when you are feeling stressed. Remember how good it felt to succeed.

Whichever kind of achievement you accomplish, big or small, give yourself a pat on the back if no one else does. When something goes well, shout 'Yes!' and punch the air, take yourself on a quick guided tour of the benefits, bask a brief while in the glory, perhaps buy yourself a little treat – a candy bar, a nice lunch or the sort of toy that appeals to you. Many of us are held back from doing this because we feel we shouldn't be blowing our own trumpet. But when there's no one else to do the trumpet blowing, don't be shy. Much stress is conquered by being in control, and control includes the ability to enjoy your successes.

This needn't be more than saying to yourself, 'that went really well' and indulging in the luxury of a big grin, but psychologically the impact is considerable. Give yourself a pat more often; you know you deserve it.

Destress 7: Get a list

I could make a very short list of people's attitudes to lists:

- Some people make lists all the time.
- Some people occasionally make lists for special occasions.
- Some people get really irritated with others who make lists.

Even if you are the sort of person who hates those irritatingly organized people who can't pack for a vacation or choose gifts without having a carefully written out list, the fact is that there are times when writing things down can help.

As we've seen, your short-term memory is pretty limited. Its capacity is seven or eight things at the most. After that, it gives up. If you try to keep everything you need to do today in your head there will be a horrible juggling act going on, as the different tasks fight for the seven or so slots of your immediate attention. At the extreme, you can get into a state similar to that of a computer with insufficient memory. It spends increasing amounts of time transferring information to and from disk. In the end, this activity takes up almost all the time – a condition that is referred to in the trade as thrashing. Most of us have been in this state where almost all your thoughts are taken up with trying to get your mental list straight.

There is only one answer: get the list on paper (or whiteboard, or computer). Put together the day's basic action list, with any outstanding tasks on a side list to make sure they don't get lost. This is not a big deal; it should only take a very few minutes. If you're the kind of person who hates making lists, you will find this exercise quite difficult. It will be easy to find something else to do instead. Fight the urge. This list will benefit even you. Some people reckon that the best time to get a task list together is in the evening, ready for the next day. However, if your mind is clearest in the morning you might find first thing better. If so, make sure that you make the list early enough to cope with anything you'll have to do.

Destress 8: Get a conversation

When you are under pressure, it's easy to see any interruption to your efforts as irritating, but small doses of regular social chat are beneficial. Apart from anything else, breaking your activity into chunks (see the next chapter) will result in less pressure and more efficiency. But the social aspect goes beyond giving you a chance to break up your work. Having a positive chat with a friend (make sure you aren't backbiting or moaning, which will increase stress) will act as a natural stress suppressor.

Have you had a chat this morning or afternoon? Make sure that you do. When you are under pressure, chatting can seem to be just a waste of time. You need to get on. You haven't time to talk. Certainly you need to control the amount of time spent chatting, but you can never be so overloaded as not to be able to spare a few minutes for social interaction. Look at it this way. If you're 150 per cent overloaded, what difference is it going to make if you turn it into 155 per cent overloaded?

We are social animals. Having a chat a couple of times a day helps make sure you break up your work and acts as a stress suppressor, as long as the conversation is positive. A phone call (or even an instant messenger chat online, if all else fails) is better than nothing, but you can't beat a face-to-face conversation.

Destress 9: Get offloaded

When things get on top of you, stress inevitably results. You need to find ways to defend yourself against overload. One way is to get your time under control (see the next chapter). Another is to offload. You could do this by delegating – which is not just for managers in an office. Don't try to do everything yourself. Ask other people to help. You can also use some little tricks to deal with the specific offloading, like dealing with a setback.

Sometimes an apparently trivial setback can really hurt. Like most writers, I have received a thick pile of rejection letters over the years. Having a book rejected may seem pretty unimportant in the grand scheme of things, but when it's an idea you've poured your heart into, rejection is very painful. The same goes for any setback. To make matters worse, failures sometimes come in clumps. It's not fate, or being jinxed; if you think about it, a series of problems wouldn't be random if they were all nice and evenly spread out. By the time you've hit your third setback in a row you can be feeling very low and very stressed.

The technique here is ancient, but it still works. If a small kid is learning to ride a bike we encourage him or her to get straight back on after a fall. Similarly, when you are hit by a setback, launch another initiative as soon as possible. This could involve a small change, be loosely related or be totally different. So, for instance, when I get a rejection on a book I might send the same proposal to a different publisher, or rework the proposal, or send out a totally different proposal addressing a different market. If you get a real downer, you can increase the reinforcement by doubling the response. If a rejection really upsets me, I send out not one proposal but two.

Timing is important. React quickly, ideally within a few hours. The knowledge that you are taking action will cut out a lot of the impact straight away. This technique demonstrates the power of anticipation. Anticipation is often better than reality. If you can set up a positive anticipation of something that equals or betters the setback, you can largely counter its impact. Of course, some setbacks are so big that nothing will counter them effectively. But for the vast majority this technique will push you back into a positive frame of mind, not giving stress a chance to take a hold.

Destress 10: Get some relaxation

We've already seen how breathing the right way can help you relax, but there are plenty of other techniques to work out that stress. Some people find that a massage or aromatherapy works for them – particularly if it's a relaxing scent in a long, warm bath. Or try this simple technique. If life is getting on top of you, find somewhere quiet where you can lie down or sit in a very comfortable chair without any distractions. Close your eyes, lie back and relax. Try to clear your mind of all thoughts.

Now focus your attention on the parts of your body, working from your head down to your toes. As you think of each bit, tense and relax the muscles a few times, holding them tense for a couple of seconds, then relaxing to a long, slow breath. Try to keep your concentration on the area you are exercising; don't let your thoughts drift off to problems or concerns.

When you have worked down the body, lie still, breathing slowly, keeping as much as possible to a mind blank of thought for another minute or so. While doing so, keep your muscles as relaxed as possible. When you have finished the exercise, don't jump up, but gently open your eyes and stand slowly. Although this technique requires somewhere you can get away from the stressful world, it can be carried out quite quickly, and is a good emergency defence when things are getting on top of you.

Another way to do this is make use of those excellent therapy centres, coffee shops and cafés. A favourite quotation that was regularly used by a very philosophical character, Wellington, in an old cartoon strip called *The Perishers* was 'What is this life if, full of care, we have no time to stand and stare?' This little snippet from the W. H. Davies poem 'Leisure' is not a bad motto for this particular exercise.

Every now and then, take yourself off to a Starbucks or whatever your preferred café or coffee shop is – preferably one with tables on the pavement. Sit down with a cup of your favourite beverage and watch the world go by. Switch off your cellphone, don't let your work or home life intrude, just soak up your environment and indulge in some people-watching. This exercise will not take long, and will amply repay the time. If you can take a coffee break away from your desk, do it.

Another thing you can do is to meditate. For some, meditation is a natural part of life; for others, it's just weird, something hippies do, not for real people. In fact, there is nothing extreme or New Age about meditation, and it doesn't require acceptance of a particular philosophy. Find somewhere you can sit quietly and comfortably. Unless you are very supple, cross-legged positions should be avoided. Reduce sensory distractions to a minimum. Breathe slowly and evenly. Imagine that everything is slowing down.

Then, find a focus. This can be a meaningless set of syllables, a simple phrase, or a very calm image like a great, unruffled lake, or a single leaf. To begin with, you may find it helps to have a physical object to provide the focus, but before long you will be able to do without it. If you use an object, don't think about any associations or properties it has – this isn't like the creativity technique where you used a leaf. Keep your focus on the entire object. For a few minutes (with your eyes closed, unless you are using something physical), let your focus fill your mind. The stress will drain away – but don't think about it, or its causes.

Initially you will find it hard to keep focused. Your mind will wander. When you notice this, bring yourself back. Don't go too long to start with. Begin with a few minutes and build up to maybe 15 minutes. Most of the world's religions, from Christianity to Zen Buddhism, and plenty of non-religious groups, practise meditation. You can see it as an opportunity to explore inner spirituality or as simple mental/physical exercise.

Whatever your view, it works. If you really have trouble with the spiritual associations, remember something the famous physicist Niels Bohr once said. He had a 'lucky' horseshoe up on his office wall. 'Surely you don't believe in such superstitious rubbish, Professor Bohr?' one of his students asked him. 'No, I don't,' said Bohr, 'but I'm told it works whether you believe in it or not.'

Meditation is hard to do without a quiet space and a few undis-turbed minutes, but its powerful impact on stress levels makes it well worth trying. Try using a timer to avoid worrying about how long you have been meditating, particularly if you have another activity to undertake later.

Chill out – essentials

Taking control of stress and understanding how your environment and your body can influence your creativity is an essential.

- Be aware of the times of day when you work best, and use those for when you need to be creative.
- Try to get away from your desk for some thinking time.
- Make the place where you work more attractive and more likely to encourage thinking.
- Keep on top of stress to help your brain get into the daydream state when required.
- Use our simple destress programme:

  - Get some sleep and some good food. Having enough sleep, watching your diet and allowing yourself occasional treats can all help.
  - Get on top of your time. Not having enough time is a constant problem. See the next chapter for more.
  - Get some air. Simple breathing exercises can help reduce stress and can be done anywhere.
  - Get a laugh. Have an emergency laughter kit and indulge in play.
  - Get physical. You may be a sports freak or hate exercise. Either way, a little applied effort can help break down stress.
  - Get a winner's trophy. Note your achievements, big and small, and give yourself a regular pat on the back.
  - Get a list. Even if you hate lists, don't get frustrated by trying to remember everything you are supposed to do today.
  - Get a conversation. You may be intensely busy, but you should always be able to spare a few minutes to chat. (Just make sure the chatting doesn't take over.)
  - Get offloaded. Don't try to do everything yourself. When hit by a setback, offload by getting straight back in there.
  - Get some relaxation. Try simple relaxation and meditation techniques. And use that great relaxer, taking time to watch the world go by.

Chapter 8

Time and time again

To study, you need all sorts of things. A brain always comes in useful, as do materials – books, a computer, websites and more. But there is one absolutely essential ingredient that doesn't always get much of a mention: it's time. You can't study without time. It's so obvious, that it can be forgotten. But unless you make sure you can deal with time properly, that studying isn't going to happen. And I don't want you just to manage your time well – I want you to be creative with it, which is, after all, what this book is about.

How much time?

Time is precious stuff that simply disappears if you don't make use of it. Just take a second to think about this. You won't get that second back. Ever. Before spending any of your time on deciding what to do about it, it's worth seeing just what you've got available. Here's a quick exercise. Note down how many hours a week you spend on the following activities. Please do this now, before reading on. You can write it on a piece of paper if you're the sort of person who doesn't like writing in books, but I suggest you live dangerously, throw caution to the wind and actually write the figures on the page, here and now (unless this is a library book).

Look at the form on the following page and then write down how many hours each week (on average) you spend on the activities listed.

Add up the total number of hours of activity you have per week. In total there are just 168 hours in a week. Not that many, really. If you have written more than 168, you either have a time machine or you are fooling yourself. Perhaps you don't get quite as much sleep as you claimed, or you don't spend quite so much time studying as you thought.

Activity	Hours per week
Sleeping	
Working/at school/at university	
Studying outside school/ university	
Eating	
Watching TV	
Hanging out with friends	
Exercising	
Playing computer/console/ board games	
Listening to music	
Travelling	
Hobbies and activities	
Anything not listed above (specify what it is):	
TOTAL	
SPARE (168 – Total)	

Check back and tweak the figures, even if you had a total of less than 168. Watch out for fooling yourself both ways. Have you cut down the amount of time you spend watching TV or hanging out with friends, because you think it sounds bad, for instance? Don't lie to yourself – no one else is going to see this, it's just for you.

If you have lots of time left over in the week, then making enough time for studying won't be a problem, though you have to ask yourself what you are doing with your life if you have so much time to spare. If you've used up every precious minute and don't have enough time for studying, something has to give. Look at what takes up most time. Can you steal a bit of time from it? What's least important? Could it lose an hour or two?

Make sure you really think about what is important to you. Sorry if this seems a bit deep for a book on studying creatively, but no pain, no gain. For instance, you will probably find you spend a fair amount of your time asleep – but having enough sleep is an essential if you are to study well, and if you want to really enjoy life. Cutting out sleep is a last resort when you are up against a deadline, and should only be done occasionally, with plenty of catch-up time afterwards.

How long at one go?

Compared with, say, being a coal miner, studying doesn't exactly come across as hard work. You sit at a desk, or in a comfy chair. You read a book, surf some websites, do a bit of writing. Call that work? You haven't even broken sweat. Of course studying isn't hard physical work, but it is genuinely heavy going for the brain. And like other parts of your body, the brain benefits from a regular rest. Keep at your studies for too long and you start to lose concentration, can't really absorb anything and generally became useless.

How long is 'too long' varies from person to person, but it's best to have a short break every 45 minutes to an hour and a half. This doesn't have to be a great long gap in your work – just five minutes is enough. It is important, though, to really get away from it all. Don't stay at the computer and play a game, or stay in the chair and read a magazine or watch TV. Get up, get out of the chair and move around. Ideally, get out of the building – get some outside, real, non-air-conditioned air.

It can seem when things are going well that there's no need for these breaks. When you are on a roll, it's difficult to stop. But even if things are going well, your ability to really work well (and particularly to work creatively) will be fading. Take a break at least every hour and a half (ideally more often), even if you don't feel like it.

Taking a break divides the work you do up into chunks. This isn't a bad thing – quite the reverse. If you've got a big project, or anything else that is going to take more than a few hours, it's really useful before plunging into it to break the job up into parts that won't take more than a couple of hours to complete. This is partly because we all like to succeed. There's a sense of achievement when you get something finished. But you need to get those successes several times a day, not every few weeks, so breaking a long project into smaller tasks makes it much more rewarding.

When I am writing a book like this it takes several months of work. I can't just sit down one lunchtime and have it all finished in time to go out in the evening. If I saw the whole book as one huge single task to be completed, it would seem impossible ever to get it finished. I'd probably be so depressed I would never start, which is a shame because I enjoy writing. Instead, I break the book down and can mentally check off achievements along the way, so I manage to reach some milestone every day. (I admit there are some days when even this seems hard, but that's life.)

One way to have regular successes every day would be to consider each chapter, and perhaps each section, as a task I had to achieve. In practice, from the way a book gets written (and thanks to word count in the word processor), it's more natural to think in terms of thousands of words. My small 'pat on the back' moments are when I pass each 1,000 word mark. And then I get a bigger sense of achievement when I reach 10,000 and 20,000 and so on. And there's also a big sense of 'getting there' when I pass the halfway mark. In this case, word count makes an ideal measure.

Breaking a big project down into pieces doesn't just help with having moments of achievement – it also gives you something to aim for. It's too much to aim for the end of the project, but if you can think, 'I'll have got somewhere if I get to point X by the end of today', or by the end of the week, then you've got a target, which is always helpful in keeping on top of your time.

The time thing also benefits from breaking up big projects into chunks, because usually you aren't just doing one thing. You might have several projects, or pieces of homework, or housework or essays or whatever, to do. By working on clear chunks you can switch from job to job after you have been doing it for a reasonable time and that way get more variety in what you do, and make progress on a number of fronts.

I'm not saying try to study five things at the same time, switching from one to the other every few seconds. But if you can do a chunk of one subject for anything from a half-hour to a couple of hours (remembering to take breaks), then switch to something different, it will help to keep you fresh.

Dealing with distractions

Have you ever sat in the middle of a field, with nothing in sight in any direction? No noise, nothing at all to distract you. It's wonderful – for about 20 seconds. Then it gets boring. We are used to living in a busy world with lots of distractions. It's great to keep in touch with mates, and catch up with your favourite soap opera or reality show – but it doesn't help get your studying completed.

I'm not saying you have to give up all these fun distractions. It's just that they can so easily take over. If you want to take control of your time, you need to make sure that the distractions occur only when you want them to.

It can be particularly bad if you are working at your computer (assuming it's connected to the internet). One minute someone will pop up on your instant messaging software for a chat. Next minute you get a noisy alert that you've had an email, and you just have to check and see who it's from. (Sadly, it's usually spam, especially when you really could do with a good distraction.)

So, make a start by turning off your instant messaging software (or switch it to 'do not disturb' mode if it has it). Then take a look at making your email software more study-friendly. Either shut it down entirely, or switch off the alerts that tell you every time a mail arrives. It doesn't mean you won't be checking your email. You can do it whenever you like, as often as you like – but you will be doing it when *you* are ready, in your time, not when the alert pings up to distract you from whatever you are doing.

Personally, I would recommend checking your email at the start or end of the regular breaks that you have to keep yourself fresh.

It's the same with your mobile (cellphone). Be daring. Switch it off while you are working and turn it back on in your breaks. That way you will stay in touch, but won't be disturbed every five minutes by a call or text message. (The same goes for your pager if you have one.) If you tend to get a lot of calls on your land line phone, disconnect it, go into a room where there isn't a phone, or get out of the house.

Other distractions are already your choice, but can still eat away at your time because it's easy to give in. Leave watching TV or getting a coffee, or whatever distraction starts to tempt you the minute you sit down to study, until one of those break periods. (Ideally, keep the TV out of everything except your long breaks like lunchtime and evening. Use a recorder to time-shift the programmes you can't miss.) Not only does putting off things like this remove the distraction, it gives you something to look forward to, which neatly leads on to the next section.

Give yourself a medal

It doesn't matter who you are, or what you do, the chances are you've got one skill honed to perfection – it's procrastination. Putting things off. We are all great at finding other things to do when we should be studying. Now think what you would do if you were trying to get a little kid to do some work for you. You'd offer him a reward – a little treat for getting the job done: some sweets, or a comic or even money. (OK, if it's your kid brother, you might offer a severe beating up if he doesn't do what you ask, but even missing out on the bruises is a sort of reward.)

This approach doesn't only work with little kids; it works with everyone. The oldest granny is a sucker for a free gift or a treat as a reward. We all are. You might think it's cheating, a trick to get some-one to do something in return for a reward that isn't worth much. But it works. And the really weird thing is, it even works when you do it to yourself. When it comes to rewards, you are just as likely to play along as anyone else is.

So if you are having trouble getting started, or keeping at your studying, plan yourself a reward. It doesn't have to be anything big. It could be 'when I finish this report I'll get myself a drink', or 'I'll have a sweet when I've read this chapter', or 'I'll listen to some music when I've finished researching my project'. Whatever the reward (and it has to be something you want to do), however small, it will help you to keep going. So don't just do your studying; give yourself a target to aim for and make sure you really do give yourself a reward.

I'm stopping at this point to get myself a cup of coffee. Not very exciting, I admit, but I was looking forward to it, and the thought of it coming along acted as a great encouragement to keep me going to the point where I'd decided to stop. It's as easy as that.

What comes first?

Nobody can do everything they need to do all at the same time. Just imagine trying – think of everything you have to do today. Now imagine trying to do it all at the same time. (I'll be generous and leave out sleeping.) You'll certainly be eating, and almost definitely travelling somewhere and talking to people. You might do some studying. You could do some other sort of work. You might see a film, or watch some TV. And so on. But there's no way you can get up in the morning and make a start on all of it at once. Even if you are great at multi-tasking, you still need to know what it is that needs doing first – it's a matter of priorities.

First of all, you can put aside the time that's scheduled – activities you have no control over the time of. It might be school or lectures. It might include a trip to the dentist or to see a play. The timing of these is outside your control. Remember, though, that this doesn't leave you entirely powerless. It's up to you to decide whether or not you do the thing at all, even if you can't change the timing – and for that, the next bit applies just as much to scheduled activities as those you choose the times for.

The tempting thing to do next, to fill in the gaps around the scheduled stuff, is to pick off the things that are easiest or most fun to do – but that's not always a good move. Really, there are two things you need to consider when deciding on what to do next: how urgent is the task, and how important is it?

You might think these are two different ways of saying the same thing – but they're not. Something urgent has to be done soon – today, maybe. But it might not be exactly life or death whether or not you do it. Something important absolutely has to be done – but not necessarily right away.

It's pretty easy to put everything you have to do into one of four boxes. (You could even use four physical file boxes if it helps, putting the different tasks in the appropriate box, but I really meant imaginary boxes.)

The first call on your time should go to the tasks that are both important and urgent. You might have an interview or an exam today. You might have a piece of crucial coursework, without which you will fail, to hand in today. Maybe you've an audition for a life-changing part, or a serious doctor's appointment. Perhaps you've a date with the most wonderful guy in the world. (Priorities are personal things, remember. But sometimes you do have to question your decision; it may be that this date isn't quite as essential when you consider its impact on the rest of your life as getting your work completed.) These are things that are essential for you to do, and that have to be done pretty well right away, and inevitably take precedence.

Next come things that are urgent but not important. These are activities that have to be done now, and you really ought to do now if at all possible, even though they aren't so important. It might be a tax return, or a competition entry, or any number of things that have to be done straight away but aren't exactly earth-shattering in importance (maybe this is where that date belongs!). Often they are admin tasks. Doing the washing up, for instance. Of course, you might decide it's so unimportant that there's no need to do it at all, but assuming it is worth doing, then get it out of the way.

If you've sorted your time well, there should be some left to catch up on what is probably the most valuable category: important but non-urgent tasks. Whenever you've got time to spare, fill in with an important non-urgent task. That way, you are trimming away the amount of work that will have to be done later with high priority when this task switches from non-urgent to urgent as the deadline draws near. Having too many important urgent tasks is what can really stress you out. The more of the important but non-urgent tasks you can get out of the way early, the less likely it is that you'll get overloaded.

Finally, there are the non-urgent, non-important things. These are tasks where there's no time pressure and, to be honest, there's not that much value in doing them. If you have four files to put your different types of task in, the file for this type of task could be called the trash can or wastepaper basket. Most of them can be junked. Not all, because some of the tasks in this category are things you really enjoy doing. (Arguably, watching TV is always a non-urgent, non-important activity, though sports fans and soap opera addicts might disagree.) But be aware when you do these activities that they shouldn't be taking priority over the important/urgent stuff.

Top Ten

A good way to get on top of what is really urgent and important for you right now is to have a top ten list. It's a simple idea, but a powerful one. Each week, write yourself a list of the top ten tasks or activities you have to do that week. It should be a series of one-line reminders of the things that are really important and urgent for you during that week. It doesn't matter if there are a few less than ten, but try not to go beyond ten. If you find yourself doing so, then either you are going into too much detail or you are trying to focus on too many different things.

During the week, there are two times when your list will come into play. If someone asks you to do something, take a glance at your list. See if what you are being asked to do will contribute to one of your top ten priorities. It doesn't mean you have to say 'no' if it doesn't, but it gives you a chance to think about whether or not you do want to go ahead, rather than plunging in and saying 'yes' without thinking.

The other time the list will be useful will be when you suddenly find yourself with some time to spare. Take a glance through your top ten list. Is there something you can do in the time you have available towards one of the items on your list? Use that list for inspiration.

Each week, check through the list and update it. Throw out some of the items and add in some new ones. If you aren't changing at least two or three items each week, your list is too general and will quickly become stale and ignored.

One final top ten tip: keep the list somewhere you can easily see it while you are working. Stick it up on the wall, or have it somewhere easily visible by your computer. A few times a day, take a glance at it, and make sure you are on track. It's a great help in managing your priorities.

Finding loose time

It's probably very childish of me, but I get really excited if I find a coin (or, even better, a banknote) on the floor. It doesn't matter if I'm the one who dropped it in the first place – it's as though I've won something. This loose change lies around the world waiting for people to pick up – and loose time is just the same. It's the little bits of time that you have lying around in your life and don't do anything with. It's amazing how much there is of it in a typical life. When you did the exercise breaking down where your time went, the chances are that you didn't allow for loose time – but it's there every day, waiting to be used.

Just think for a minute of all those spare moments that slip down the back of the sofa of time (if you see what I mean). When you're on a bus or waiting for the bus. When you are waiting for anything, in fact. Those bits of time when it's not worth starting anything big, but you've a few minutes to spare. If only you could stick them all together, they would make quite a chunk of your life. And you also have to remember that time has a limited shelf life. Once a particular minute has gone by, you can't come back to it a few weeks later. You need, as some movie or other once said, to seize the day.

Aside: Seize the day

This is advice that has been around a long time (certainly well before Robin Williams came out with it in *Dead Poets Society*). Over two thousand years ago the Roman poet Horace came up with the line 'Carpe diem, quam minimum credula postero', or 'Seize the day, put no trust in the future'. The seventeenth-century poet Robert Herrick used the same idea in his poem 'To the Virgins, to Make Much of Time' when he said, 'Gather ye rosebuds while ye may', though his intentions were rather less lofty.

OK, you can't stick your spare minutes together the way you can collect up loose change – but you can do something with them. One bit of advice I find really useful was given to me by the British comedian Dave Thompson. Dave is never without his notebook, ready to use those spare moments to jot down the beginnings of a joke, a little bit of overheard conversation, anything that comes to mind. I always try to do the same now, though my 'notebook' could be just the back of a supermarket till receipt, or a voice recorder on my PDA.

When you've a minute or two to spare, think of something you need to do – it might be to do with study, it might be something you do for fun. Jot down a few notes so that when you have more time to give to it, you can do it better. If you've a few minutes to spare sitting at your PC, instead of playing a game on the internet, pick off one of the tasks you've still got left to do. If you can get it out of the way in this 'dead' time, you can save it eating into a larger piece of time when you can do something more worthwhile.

It might seem as though this is a recipe for rushing around, always frantic, never taking a break. Not at all. Having breaks is part of using your time properly. But picking up loose time is a way to cut down on the time you waste. Let's say you live to the age of 80. That means you've about 42 million minutes in your life, of which a fair number have already gone. Every one you throw away, you'll never get back. Doesn't it make sense to do something with those spare minutes, rather than waste them?

Saying 'no'

One little word is extremely powerful when it comes to time. It's 'no'. Most of us like to please our friends; many of us go further and set out to please just about anyone around. That's good, uplifting and very civic minded. But it won't help you get your studying done. Sometimes the best thing to do is to say 'no'.

Of course, you don't need to be that blunt. Just saying 'no' and nothing else won't win you any friends. The best way to make a 'no' less offensive is to attach something else to it. So if your mates want to go out when you are in the middle of something you really need to finish, you can say 'No, I can't make it right now, but how about doing it . . .' Give them an alternative.

Apart from anything else, setting up an alternative could be the only way of saving you from yourself. If someone asks you to do something you really enjoy when you should be studying, immediately you can feel yourself thinking, 'it won't really matter', or 'it's only an hour or two', or whatever. And before you know it, you've given in. Saying 'no' is sometimes about taking charge of yourself and making a bargain with yourself that you will have this to look forward to, but you really need to get your work finished first.

In other cases it could be that you don't really want to do what someone is asking anyway. Then you've a double reason to say 'no'. In cases like this, try to make sure that the person who is after your time (think of them as time vampires if you want to make this personal) is let down gently but firmly. Saying 'yes' will waste your time and will make you miserable. Saying 'no, but we'll do it another time' just puts off the evil day. It's best to say, 'thanks for asking me, but it's really not my thing' or whatever and put a permanent stop to it, otherwise it will just come back to haunt you.

Expect the unexpected

If there were a prize for the dumbest-sounding words of wisdom ever uttered, it ought to go to 'expect the unexpected'. This is about on a par with 'you have nothing to fear but fear itself' in the supreme stupidity stakes. Obviously you can't expect the unexpected or it wouldn't be, er, unexpected. But you can give it breathing space to act in. You can't expect the specific thing that turns up, but you certainly can expect that it will. And you won't be disappointed.

One of the biggest problems with getting any kind of work done – school work, business, DIY, whatever – is the unexpected disturbance. However cleverly you manage your time, sometimes something will go wrong.

Dealing with the unexpected means having two handy weapons available to help cope. The first is buffers. These are chunks of time you reserve around something you are doing to allow for the fact it might take a little longer than expected. So if you've two pieces of work that should take an hour each, allow two and a half hours, or something like that, to make sure you can cover most eventualities. Don't fill up your schedule – whether it's a revision schedule for examinations, or meetings, or your work, or your travel plans – so that every minute of the day is crammed with activity. Leave some spare capacity for when things go pear-shaped.

Second, have an emergency exit and know where it is.

Aside: Emergency exits

Every evening in hotels around the globe, careful observers will see a strange little ritual happening. Airline crew will come out of their hotel room, find the nearest emergency exit, check that they can get out of it, and count doors between the exit and their bedroom. It's part of their training. As they spend a lot of time in hotels, and hotel fires can be horrendous, they go through this little drill so they can get out in an emergency. When the place is full of smoke and the alarms are going off, it's too late to go hunting for the emergency exit. All too often, you arrive on your floor in a lift that can't be used in an emergency – and have no idea how to get out.

This is something you should consider doing when you stay in a hotel. The first thing after getting to your room, just spend a minute finding the emergency exit. Visualize getting to

> it in thick smoke. It just might save your life. (The same goes for the next time you are on a plane.) But it's also a good example of the second half of expecting the unexpected: knowing what to do if things go wrong.

When I say, 'have an emergency exit', unless you are in a hotel room or on a plane this might not be literally what we're talking about. The point is to know what to do if things go catastrophically wrong.

Take a simple example. I live about a one-hour train journey from London. If I have a meeting in the city, I'll catch a train that will get me there about an hour before my meeting is due. That's my buffer.I can always make use of the time (I carry stuff with me to do, and I can sit in a café at the station with a cup of coffee, working comfortably until it's time for the meeting). But by having that buffer, I can cope if there are problems getting to the station, or if the train is delayed, which isn't too unusual.

My emergency exit in this example is that I will have a cellphone with me, and have the number of the person I'm meeting programmed in, so if there should be an even bigger problem – the train breaks down, for instance – I can call them up, explain the delay and reschedule. I also have enough working material with me to keep busy throughout the day if necessary.

The same approach can apply to any important task, including your studying. Build in some buffer time to allow for the unexpected. And know what to do if it all goes horribly wrong and you aren't going to be able to complete your task.

Time and time again – essentials

One of the most common problems in studying is managing the time you have properly. But it doesn't have to be difficult.

- Get a better feel for the time you have available and be honest about how you want to use it.
- Break up your tasks into 45-minute to one-hour chunks. Don't go past one and a half hours without a break.
- Do something different (get away from the computer and out of the building if possible) in short breaks between working.

- Set yourself milestones to aim for, and make sure you have achievements you can manage in a short period of time, so you can succeed today and every day.
- Do something about distractions. Don't think you can work around your phone calls, emails and instant messages.
- Reward yourself for making it through a task.
- Get your priorities straight: urgent and important things first, then urgent (but not too many of these), then important. As much as possible, bin the non-urgent, non-important tasks.
- Have a top ten list of tasks and activities you really want to get done this week. Update it each week and use it.
- Make use of spare minutes. You only live once.
- Learn how to say 'no' without irritating people.
- Manage the unexpected by allowing buffer time and by knowing what to do if it all goes horribly wrong.

Chapter 9

Creativity zone

The chapters so far have introduced a whole range of techniques you can use to help you be more creative in your study. But it's not enough to know what the techniques are; you need to be able to make them part of your normal routine. The last two sections look away from the techniques themselves and look more at what you actually need to *do*. This chapter concentrates on pulling the techniques into your working life. The next provides a set of resources to help you go further with developing and supporting your creativity.

Remember the wheel nuts

A while back, I mentioned the idea of someone trying to take wheel nuts off with their bare hands. It seems stupid, but they do it because they think they don't have time to go and get the right tool for the job. As you move away from this book and back to day-to-day work, whether it's studying or whatever else you do, it's so easy to slip into that attitude: that you are too busy to find and use the right tool. You will try to take wheel nuts off with your bare hands. Consider sticking up a notice to remind yourself not to do this.

10 a.m. – time to be creative

The first practical suggestion I have for getting creativity into your life sounds a little off the wall. I want you to put 'being creative' in your diary. (You don't have a diary? Either get one or start using the diary on your computer. No wonder you're stressed.)

This is a thought that really upsets some people. You know the type. (If you are this type of person, this isn't personal; bear with me.) They have to be in just the right mood to work. The muse has to be with them. 'It's not something you can switch on and off', they say.

When the creative spirit takes you, it's there. The rest of the time it isn't. I'm sorry, but this is garbage, pure and simple.

Some writers claim to suffer from writer's block, which is an extreme example of this 'moved by the spirit' creativity. There is no such thing.

I don't deny there are times when we're better at having good ideas than at other times (see page 102). All the creativity techniques in the world won't guarantee having a great idea. But creativity is something we can all do, all the time. A lot of the 'writer's block' problem is either procrastination – putting things off – or laziness. It's a very natural response. I love writing. It's something I do every day, and I really enjoy it. Yet just take a look at my typical activities first thing in the morning.

I'll check for urgent emails, then have breakfast, then check the snail mail and a few essential websites. Then I'll check my emails again. I might have to go down to the post office, and take the dog for a walk (we both need the exercise). By now it's about 10.30 and so far I haven't written a single word. If I'm honest, I really, really don't want to start. Yet as soon as I do force myself to begin writing, I love it. I rattle away and find it really hard to stop. I wonder why I ever put off getting started. Then next morning I will do exactly the same thing.

I genuinely don't understand why I put off something that I find so enjoyable. But if it's true of me – and I love writing – you can see how getting started can be a nightmare for people who don't love what they do. Famously, the sadly missed writer of hilarious science fiction Douglas Adams always put off writing till well after the last minute. He was still finishing off scripts while his original radio series was being recorded. To get books written, his publisher had to lock him in his hotel room, sending in regular food parcels, until he produced the goods. He was an extreme case, but it's a problem we all have.

So what I recommend is putting a small space in your diary – try half an hour a week – when you are going to be creative. Schedule it in your peak *with it* time. You can use this space to come up with new ideas, to solve problems, to look at things differently. You can also use this time to learn a bit more about being creative. Learn a new memory technique. Try out speed reading. Use one of the brain-stretching exercises I covered in Chapter 2. But whatever you do, it has to be creative time; it's not just an opportunity to finish off an overdue assignment.

Make sure you try out at least one technique each time. But remember, the forces of procrastination will fight back. You will try to put it off. You will realize you had something else to do. You will struggle like a dog facing a bath. Don't let the anti-creative forces win. Do something, and do it regularly. It's important that this isn't something you do just once, then give up. Creativity becomes so much easier with repeated practice. The more practice you get at coming up with new ideas, the easier it becomes.

Take charge of your time

Although the suggestions in Chapter 8 on dealing with time play only a supporting role in helping you to be more creative, you can also look at them as the foundation you are going to build on. Getting a sense of organization in how you manage your time is essential if you are going to make room for creativity.

If you are the kind of person who rebels at lists and structures and wants creativity to be all fluffy and unrestrained, I haven't got good news for you. You don't have to go mad with your time management, but unless you take some sort of charge of your time, everyone and everything else's demands will take over and you will never get what you want done finished.

To be creative you need to open up some space and some time to work in. You need to have the freedom to be able to use a technique or to take a walk, or whatever it takes. If you are on a constant tread-mill, you aren't able to do that. So get in charge of your time before going any further.

Once you have your time under better control, consider expanding that creative time slot from half an hour to half a day. That's what the company 3M does. Employees are encouraged to spend half a day a week working on something creative and different from their every-day job. If a hard-nosed, money-minded company like 3M can spare half a day a week, so can you.

Change the way you take notes

If you haven't done so already, the next thing that's worth doing is to overhaul your note taking. Give mind mapping a try. Use it for a week or two before deciding whether or not it's really for you. If, after that, it isn't working and you return to conventional notes, make sure you are making the most of your layout, highlighting and illustrating.

Look for creativity triggers

Even the most creative person doesn't spend their entire life running around having great ideas every single moment of the day. If there had been soap operas back then, it wouldn't have surprised me if Einstein had taken time off to sit back and watch something relaxing before dashing off another theory. (He always claimed to be a very lazy person.)

This book gives you techniques that will help you be more creative and come up with good ideas. You should be aware of the triggers that suggest you need to use one of these techniques. Of course there will be your weekly creativity session (you have put that in your diary, haven't you? If not, do it now!) – but you should also think of creativity when you are starting on a new project, have something to write like an essay or dissertation, or have a problem to solve, whether it's part of your study or in real life.

These are all external triggers – things out there in the world that say, 'we need an idea'. But be aware also that there are some triggers that come from inside. You might be taking a walk, or in the shower (or any of the other ways you can get into that thoughtful, creative state), when you suddenly think, 'Hey, wouldn't it be a great idea to . . .' Don't let those personal triggers escape. Make sure you've some way of noting your ideas down; carry a notebook or a voice recorder. When you get to your weekly creativity session, check those notes for anything worth working on. You might have an idea that could transform your life, or just one that results in a little fun. Either way, it was worth hanging on to it.

Take another look at your presentation

When you've a minute to spare – perhaps in the next creativity slot in your diary – take a look at the work you've done recently. Come at it with a fresh eye. Imagine you are someone else. What do you think of it? What's good about it and what's bad about it? Think about my suggested presentation rules. Have you kept yourself down to two fonts per document, and readable ones at that? Have you avoided background colours that don't work with the text?

Then take a read through the text. Does it read well, making you think 'this is great', or is it clumsy? Could you imagine reading this in a book or a magazine? If not, what's missing that would make it professional writing? Check back to Chapter 3 for tips on making your text more readable.

Read more, but read differently

Studying always involves a lot of reading, and often, frankly, it's dull. The thought of reading textbooks and academic papers, particularly, rarely makes anyone whoop with excitement. Yet I'm going to tell you that you should read more.

Before you groan and throw this book at the wall, I need to clarify that a bit. I want you to read more, but to read differently. First of all, make sure you've had a go at the speed reading exercises in Chapter 6. Next, look for some different reading matter. Reading something that's interesting and exciting is a positive boost for your creativity.

Two types of book I'd particularly recommend for giving the brain a boost are popular science and science fiction. Popular science may be non-fiction, but it's nothing like the stuff you get in science text-books. Good popular science books bring out the sense of wonder and discovery in science, and make it fun. They challenge you to think about things, which makes them great exercise for the brain. See www.popularscience.co.uk for recommendations on what's best in the popular science field.

Science fiction works in a similar way. OK, the science here might be made up (though a lot of SF makes use of ideas from real science), but, almost uniquely, it's a form of fiction driven by ideas rather than characters, and that is what you need for creative inspiration. I'm particularly talking about science fiction books here. TV shows and movies, with some notable exceptions, tend to be much weaker. See www.infinityplus.co.uk for recommended reading in this field.

If you already read a lot in both these areas, try another type of book that will still challenge you to think. A well-written history, for instance. Whichever type you choose, don't look on this as reading for a worthy reason like studying; this is pure brain food and fun.

Make sure you are chilling out

You might think of the 'chilling out' part of this book as an optional extra. You've got the real parts to help you study, then the chilling out, which is just a bit of fluffy rubbish to make studying creatively appear cool. Nothing could be further from the truth. Without this, all the rest hasn't much chance of surviving. As Chapter 7 makes clear, stress is a real problem, and one that will damage creativity. You may think you are totally stress-free – but if you are rushing around from one thing to another, under pressure, you aren't going to perform at your best.

Just as the idea of trying to take wheel nuts off with your bare hands shows that you need to take the time to think about creativity, it also shows that you need to be able to relax a little, take a step back from the problem and think more easily. Of course, some people genuinely aren't stressed. Everything comes easy to them. There are no pressures as far as they are concerned. But such people are few and far between. (And, sad to say, the rest of us hate them.)

Studying creatively

All this stuff about creativity is here for a reason – actually, for a whole raft of reasons. It's going to make what you produce better. Your essays or homework. Your dissertation or project. It's going to help you solve problems, wherever they crop up. And it's going to make what you do more enjoyable. When you can put something really original into your work, it's so much more fun to do than it is to just keep plodding away doing the same old thing.

You could look at creativity as more work. After all, you had to read this book – isn't that working? But that would miss the point. Studying creatively isn't about working harder, it's about working smarter. And that can't be a bad thing.

Appendix
Creativity resources

Studying Creatively is a starting point. It might be all you ever need – but there are plenty of other resources out there if you want to do more to help your creativity. Many of these resources are aimed at businesses – but that really doesn't matter. Creativity is the same whatever you are doing with it.

A useful central resource is my *Creativity Unleashed* website, www.cul.co.uk. This contains free software, links to other websites, articles on creativity, and much more. Again, the principal target is business, but that's not a problem. Pages you might find particularly useful are these:

- www.cul.co.uk/info.htm – this is the information site home page, taking you to book reviews, articles, software, etc., whereas the main home page is more about training for business.
- www.cul.co.uk/writers – if your interest in creativity is particularly about writing – perhaps you want to become an author – these are resources specifically aimed at the writer.

I've pulled out a few of the links and recommendations below.

Creativity online

As well as the information site at www.cul.co.uk, take a look at:

- www.brainstorming.co.uk – lots of information on creativity
- www.creativeideas.org.uk – a simple but well-stocked creativity site
- www.gocreate.com/workouts – a collection of articles on creativity

Books to help with creativity

There are loads of books in our online review, but here are some favourites:

- *Thinkertoys*, Michael Michalko (Ten Speed Press, 2006) – a large-format, striking book with lots of exercises and mechanisms for encouraging creativity. There is just too much in it for an end-to-end read, but it works very well if you divide it up, using each chapter say on a daily basis. Where this book really wins is its techniques for improving individual creativity, helping the individual break down the barriers that get in the way of personal innovation. When it comes to this, it's simply the best.
- *A Whack on the Side of the Head*, Roger von Oech (Warner, 1990) – an old one but a good one in this zany but very practical US West Coast approach to creativity.
- *How to Mind Map*, Tony Buzan (HarperCollins, 2002) – Tony Buzan, who invented the term 'mind map' and popularized cognitive mapping, has written many books on mind maps. This is probably the best one to go for.

Creativity software

Creativity software is harder to recommend without more information than I can provide here. Take a look at the reviews at www.cul.co.uk/software.

Puzzles, problems and mind stretching

For puzzles online, take a look at Aha! Puzzles (www.ahapuzzles.com) and Word Juxtapoz (www.wordjuxtapoz.com).

If you prefer your puzzles in book form, try:

- *Test Your Creative Thinking*, Lloyd King (Kogan Page, 2003). A good collection of creative problem-solving exercises and tests designed to help you exercise your mental muscles.
- *Sit and Solve Lateral Thinking Puzzles*, Des MacHale and Paul Sloane (Sterling, 2003). Lateral thinking puzzles provide a great way to tone up the mental muscles, but few us can sensibly schedule time for dedicated puzzle solving. This delightful little book suggests a way around this. As the shape of the book (a

toilet seat) suggests, we've all got daily thinking time when we can fit in a puzzle or two.

- *Mind-Bending Lateral Thinking Puzzles*, Nick Hoare and Simon Melhuish (Lagoon, 1995). A little, pocket-sized book of puzzles you can take anywhere with you and use to give your brain some exercise in any spare minute.

More on a different kind of reading

As we've seen, books can make all the difference to creativity. The more widely you read, the more it is going to help you make new connections and come up with new ideas. Read fiction and non-fiction. Sometimes choose something you wouldn't imagine reading normally, just for the creative fun of it. The short story below illustrates a point on the 'Being someone else' technique on page 27, but it's also having a bit of fun by taking an unusual viewpoint.

Observations

It's not easy being a nasturtium. There's no conversation from you lot. I mean, someone might say, 'what a pretty nasturtium' as they look round the garden, but that hardly constitutes intellectual stimulus. Anyway, it smacks of being the horticultural equivalent of a sex object, a centrefold flower; they certainly aren't interested in me for my mind.

If you're wondering how I know what they say, there's nothing wrong with my hearing. It's obvious I can't see – I haven't got eyes, have I? – but I hear perfectly well. Vibrations in the stamens, quite a sensitive pick-up with a big bell horn like . . . oh, compost, here comes a bee. I don't mind it in principle, it's all good natural stuff, but when it gets inside it tickles horribly. And I can't help feeling violated, you know? Ooh, careful there. These bumble bees are so clumsy; give me a honey bee any day. Where was I? Oh, yes, the senses. You don't have to feel sorry for me because I can't see. I smell too – not like a rose smells, snailbrain, I mean I have a sense of smell; I feel touch and I'm sensitive to a whole range of the electromagnetic spectrum. It doesn't give me that prissy, focused clarity that the eye seems to have, but I can interpret the shapes pretty well and I see your heat and the radio noise from your motors – all sorts of things beyond your vision.

I can understand it coming as a bit of a shock, finding out that a plant is sentient, but don't go jumping to conclusions. The whole garden isn't teeming with intellect. You don't hear great debates coming from the herbaceous border or poetry emerging from a holly bush. It's only us nasturtiums that are different and that's because we aren't really plants; not as you expect them to be. We didn't evolve like this. Well, I suppose we did evolve, unless our fundamentalists are right and we were created by a supreme shrub from a drop of his ineffable nectar, but what I'm trying to say is that we didn't evolve in the sunny gardens of suburbia from a perfectly ordinary rootstock.

Incidentally, what does 'ineffable' mean? It's the sort of garbage I hear all the time. I only got planted next to a Jehovah's Witness, didn't I? You can't imagine what it's like, being asked every morning if you've thought about God lately. I can't get away; I've twisted my stem as much as I can in an attempt to get behind that cracked flowerpot on the patio, but the evil hybrid follows me. He's not really a Jehovah's Witness – I mean, he's a nasturtium, after all – but he would be if he were human. The only advantage I've got over you when you get caught at the front door in your pyjamas at ten o'clock on a Saturday morning is that he can't sell me a copy of the *Watchtower*. No hands.

And I still don't know what ineffable means. It sounds like swearing somehow, but it feels more like a smell. I asked him once outright, old God Squad, and he came up with a perfect circular argument. God's nectar is ineffable. What does ineffable mean? It means having the nature of God's nectar, of course. Very enlightening. He moved quickly on to the bit of scripture that shows (according to him) that only the few will be saved and packeted up in a seed bag for the second coming.

How did I get on to this? Evolution, wasn't it? Prepare yourself for a shock: we are not of this world. I know you say the same about Jehovah's Witnesses, but that's not what I mean; I mean we're extraterrestrial. Not like ET, I don't go around wanting to phone home or anything; this is home. I suppose you're wondering how I know about ET. I can't claim to be an expert on Spielberg, but I do enjoy a classic movie. It's the girl, you see, the one from the house. When the weather's good she brings one of those little portable TV things out on to the lawn and when it's not so good she has the window wide open. She always watches the movies, and I can always tell which one she is – though a lot of nasturtiums couldn't.

To be frank – and it's embarrassing, because I'm talking about my own kind – nasturtiums are people-ist. They say things like 'they all look the same to me', and 'they're only animals, after all', and they call you blubberies and clodhoppers and other terms of abuse. It isn't fair, because once you get to know people they're quite different from one another; maybe not as individual as nasturtiums, but they have marked traits. I'm sure you have too. And I know it's not true that you all live by eating animal flesh; that's a foul distortion put around by extremists. As for all being the same, I can often tell what sex someone is without even using my sense of smell.

Sex – now that's something I'll never understand. Like I said, I can relate intellectually to bees, but who could enjoy it? Enjoyment's another thing entirely. And yet humans let their whole lives be dominated by an obsession with sex. I suppose that's why they don't have such a rich and contemplative culture as our own. They're too busy worrying about the opposite sex to give much thought to art. Certainly that's the case if the TV's anything to go by. Mind you, sex never seems to happen in our back yard, unless you count that little incident behind the shed; I never really got to the bottom of that.

We, of course, live our art. We are our art, in fact. I don't mean the coloured petals – a pretty face is a pretty face, art doesn't come into it – but the shapes we describe as we grow can be the highest form of expression. That's if you aren't more concerned about avoiding your fundamentalist neighbour than adding a third counter-spiral to your main stem. That idiot is personally responsible for my lack of cultural development; I should sue him.

Hello, here comes the cat again. I suppose they seem fun to you, just furry little bundles, but from down here the world is very different. You never know when you're going to be sprayed with some foul-smelling fluid or half dug up to make room for more sordid waste products. That's one thing you animals have never got right. We mostly pump out oxygen; it's invisible, odour free and generally regarded as useful. What did you ever find to do with cat poop?

Ah. No problem, it was just following the scent of a bird that passed through early, no doubt after the proverbial worm. We nasturtiums have proverbs too, but I have to say it is one area where humanity seems to have the edge. 'Too many cooks spoil the broth' and 'people who live in glass houses shouldn't throw stones' don't have much competition from 'too many leaves makes for poor petals except when the soil is particularly rich or weather conditions unusually favourable'. Nasturtium literature is not famous for pithiness.

I haven't really explained about us being extraterrestrial, have I? You might have wondered why it's so easy to grow nasturtiums; how you've only got to show us a bit of soil and we bounce up all over the place. The thing is, when your seeds are used to entering the Earth's atmosphere and plummeting in free fall without so much as a thistledown parachute and slamming into any old bit of soil, you've got to be adaptable.

Not that we all are. Some nasturtiums have become very fussy. It's the political activists, you see. You probably put it down to the wrong sort of soil or not enough water and sun: something suitably environmental. Anthers to that. They're stroppy buggers, that's what it is. They come out of their seeds demanding certain rights and they're not going to grow unless they get them. And since no one but us other poor, uncomplaining nasturtiums gets to hear them, nothing gets done and they die sorry deaths.

Death's a difficult one, of course. Life and death; water and drought. I mean, forgetting old second coming next door, it's a bit of a puzzler. We don't hang around for long in human terms, I can see that. At least, I assume you're telling the truth, but maybe it's like sex: everyone lies about it so much that no one's sure what the truth really is. What I do know is that we come into this world well endowed with genetic memory, and by the time we're flowering, we're adults (my neighbour apart). Then along comes autumn, whatever that is, and zap, you've had it. It makes you think. Couldn't someone do away with autumn?

I'm churning all this into my root structure and I don't suppose any of you humans are going to have the intelligence to decode it, but you've got to leave something for posterity. Even if you could decode it, I suppose it'd be considered a hoax. I mean, you aren't entirely receptive to the concept of intelligent plants from another planet. That said, there was the John Wyndham business, but really! I certainly wouldn't want to share a bed with a triffid, would you? It's downright exploitation of plants. It's not us who go around mangling and eating other creatures. OK, so there are a few carnivores among us, but they're the black sheep of the family. You never see a carnivorous plant at a garden party or a wedding, do you?

What I'm trying to say is, don't go bracketing us with triffids in your mind. Let's face it, they were pretty unlikely, weren't they? Isn't there too much suspension of disbelief required to cope with a dirty great stinging plant that can walk? Humans can take a lot away from us, but not the dignity of immobility. I should imagine a triffid would look positively ludicrous. But wait, what vibrations through yonder garden path echo? It is the east and some human or other is the sun. I draw the line at calling you clodhoppers, but I have to agree you're heavy-footed. It's like a small earthquake, it is.

You'll have noticed the subtle literary reference there, unless you read the newspaper that is convinced that Elvis is still singing somewhere on the dark side of the moon. It may come as some surprise to you to know that I have a wide and incisive knowledge of *Complete William Shakespeare Revision*. Of course, Revision was one of your greatest writers, so maybe even the scandal sheet readers would have heard of him. He may well have worked on *Saturday Night Live* back in the early days.

Whatever, Revision must have been a great man to become famous with a name like that. My expert knowledge originates from the girl in the house, who was reading up for examinations back in my youth. She used to sprawl on the grass with her coursebook and read vast chunks of Revision's greatest hits out loud. I can't help but suspect he was a nasturtium himself. Not only was he unusually intelligent for a human, but he had the nasturtium way of never using two words when ten will do.

But this is distracting from my reportage of the present. It's not the girl this time, it's the other female, the one with the more extensive clothing. Probably got something to hide: we nasturtiums say, 'if you've got it, flaunt it', or, more precisely, 'if you have the sort of petals that make you stand out in the crowd or if you have a beautifully formed stem, get out from under that cloche and stun the lot of them', which as usual lacks conciseness. She's coming right up to us; bending over the bed.

I know you make a lot of fuss about faces, but really they are the most unattractive blurs. I think the human race would be a lot better off if it concentrated more on ankles. From here, I'd say that they were your best feature. But anyway, she's thrusting this blobby face thing at me. The eyes are most odd, they change the light in a distressing way. She's feeling me up! The cheek of it; what sort of pervert is she? She's running her fingers over my petals. Give me a bee any time, this is downright unpleasant. Now she's . . . ouch.

I really don't know what to say. She's only pulled my head off. I'm not going to be able to add much more; I don't need to be physically connected to the stem to code my roots, but I can't live long like this. What's the big idea? I see them cutting flowers, the flashy numbers like the roses, but at least they have the grace to leave them a bit of stem. She just twisted my head straight off. The only consolation, if it's possible to be consoled when you've had your head pulled off, is that she got the Jehovah's Witness too. Let's see him be holier than thou now, eh.

Mostly I can only see sky, though she's joggling us around. Lots of sky . . . then a wall – so that's what's behind the shed. What's this? We're going into the house. I know all about houses, but I've never seen one; perhaps she's feeling remorse and she's going to show me round before I pop off. She's turning me over a bit; I can see ahead. Oh no. This is too much. I demand a refund. How would you like to end up as a garnish on a salad? I could curl up and . . .

Extract from 'Observations from an Electron Microscope Study: A Nasturtium's Roots Decoded' by Dr John D. Rapley, an article rejected by Nature *shortly before Dr Rapley's unfortunate involuntary incarceration in the Reebeck Institute for the Criminally Deranged.*

Index

achievements 112–13, 122
adrenaline 107
advertising, creativity in 2
alcohol 109
associations, of picture 18
attributes technique 23
audio notes 72
available time in week 119–20

being-someone-else technique 27–9
bibliographies 51
blocking creativity 12–15
books, creativity *see* creativity
box, thinking outside the 6
brain, halves of 7; left and right 8;
    percentage used 10
brains 6–10; brains versus
    computers 79
brainstorming 6
breaks 121
breathing 3, 109–10
buffer time 131
Buzan, Tony 69

categories 50, 71–2
chains, for memory *see* memory
    chains
characters 27–8
chronological structure 49
citations 51
colour, use in notes 68

colours 58–9
columns 52
computerized note taking 73
conclusions 50
contents page 50
conversation 114–15
corpus callosum 7
creativity books 140; software 31;
    triggers 136; websites 139
criticism of ideas 13
culture 4

da Vinci, Leonardo 3
daydreaming 106–7
de Bono, Edward 32
declarative memory 79
delegating 115
desks 104–5
diet 108–9
differentiation 2
distractions, avoiding 16, 123–4

embarrassment 15
email 123
emergency exits 130–1
endorphins 107
energy boosting 30
environment 4, 104–5
epinephrine 107
exercise 111–12
experts 14

fonts 55
Freemind 75–6
fun 5, 110–11

Google 17
green shoots 14
guide, use in reading *see* visual
    guide

habitual phrases 61
highlighters 69
horror stories 25

idea generating 2
image search 18
Imagination Engineering 44
introductions 50, 100
italics 57

justification of text *see* text
    justification

Land, Edwin 14
lateral thinking 32
laughter 110–11
layout, of notes 68; of page *see* page
    layout
leaf 45
line spacing 53
lists 113–14
logic problems 32
long-term memory 79

Man Who Stopped Time, The 49
meditation 117
metaphors 3, 43–4
memory 78–94
memory chains 87
MindManager 76
mind map software 75–6
mind maps 69–71, 135
Muybridge, Eadweard 49

names, remembering 89–91

nasturtiums 141–6
neurons 7
no, saying 129
notes 51, 66–77
numbers, remembering 80–6
number rhymes 83–5
number shapes 85–6

Observations 141–6
one-off project, information for 67
OneNote 74–5
outlines 49

padding 63
page layout 52
PDAs 73, 128
personalizing work 48–9
pi, memorizing 81–2
picture, choosing 17; random *see*
    random picture technique
pictures 54
play 110–11
Polaroid camera 14
PowerPoint 88–9
practice 5
presentation, memorizing 87–9
pressure 10, 105–18, 137–8
prioritization 125–6
problem solving 2
procedural memory 79
procrastination 134–5
pronouns 60–1
puzzles 32–41, 140–1
Pygmalion effect 12

random picture technique 17–23
reading 95–101, 137, 141; from
    screens 98–9
recaps 91–2
relaxation 116–17
resources 139–41
reversal technique 25
rewards 124
rhymes, for memory 81

rules in creativity 25

sans serif fonts 55–6
scheduled creativity 133–5
screen display of text 63–5
screens, reading from *see* reading
script, memorizing 87–9
secret, hiding a 41–2
self-esteem 112–13
self-patterning systems 91–2
sentence length 60
serif fonts 55–6
shooting down ideas 14
short stories 44–5, 46
short-term memory 79
skim reading 99–101
sleep 107–8
software for creativity *see* creativity
someone else technique *see* being
    someone else technique
speed reading 95–7
squirreled information 67
stories *see* short stories
stories as memory aids 86–7
stress 10–11, 105–18, 137–8
Stroop effect 8–9
structure of documents 49–52
Studying Using the Web 51, 62

StumbleUpon 30

tablet PCs 73
tasks 122
teams and creativity 6
techniques 4–6, 12
telephone numbers 80
text justification 52
time management 119–32
titles 52
top ten list 126–7
tunnel vision 6
TV 123–4

underlining 57
unexpected, expecting the 129–30
use of colour *see* colours

visual guide 95–6

walking, for creativity 16; for stress
    relief 112
websites, creativity *see* creativity
    websites
wheel nuts, taking off 30–1
with-it index 102–3
writers' block 134
writing things down 22